WORD 97

Moira Stephen

TEACH YOURSELF BOOKS

Orders: please contact Bookpoint Ltd, 39 Milton Park, Abingdon, Oxon OX14
4TD. Telephone: (44) 01235 400414, Fax: (44) 01235 400454. Lines are open
from 9.00 – 6.00, Monday to Saturday, with a 24 hour message answering
service. Email address: orders@bookpoint.co.uk

British Library Cataloguing in Publication Data
A catalogue record for this title is available from The British Library

ISBN 0-340-70493-4

First published 1998
Impression number   10 9 8 7 6 5 4 3 2
Year   2004 2003 2002 2001 2000 1999 1998

The 'Teach Yourself' name and logo are registered trade marks of Hodder &
Stoughton Ltd.

Typeset by MacDesign, Southampton
Printed in Great Britain for Hodder & Stoughton Educational,
a division of Hodder Headline Plc, 338 Euston Road, London NW1 3BH
by Cox & Wyman Ltd, Reading, Berkshire.

CONTENTS

1

GETTING STARTED

1.1 Aims of this chapter

This chapter introduces the word processing package Word 97. We will start with an overview of the package, and move on to consider the hardware and software required to run Word 97 successfully. We then look at how you install the package on your computer. Getting into Word 97, the working environment, on-line Help system and exiting Word 97 will also be discussed.

1.2 Introducing Word 97

Word 97 is a very powerful word processing package – but don't let that put you off! It can be used to create simple letters, memos and reports – you'll soon discover how easy it is to generate these. You can use its more sophisticated features to produce mail shots, forms, newsletters and multi-page publications. Word integrates well with the rest of the Office suite, so you can create professional documents that combine files generated in other applications. And Word 97 is Web orientated – you can hyperlink to documents and Internet addresses, send e-mails and publish on the Web!

1.3 Hardware and software

To run Word 97 successfully on your computer, it should meet the following minimum hardware and software specifications. The first set gives the system requirements for Word 97 only, the second set gives details of additional requirements should you be installing the entire Microsoft Office suite.

SPECIFICATION FOR WORD 97

PC	486 or higher
Operating System	Windows 95 or Windows NT Workstation version 3.51 Service Pack 5 or later
RAM	A minimum of 8 Mb for Windows 95; 16 Mb for Windows NT Workstation
Hard Disk space	Between 20 Mb and 60 Mb. A typical installation requires 42 Mb
CD-ROM Drive	The package normally comes on CD (you have to ask for the diskette version if you want it). The CD version is quicker to install and has additional components, e.g. Microsoft Internet Explorer, extra Clip Art, video files and sound files
Disk Drive	One 3.5" High Density disk drive (if you've bought the diskette version)
Monitor	VGA or higher resolution video adapter (SVGA 256 colour recommended)
Mouse	Microsoft mouse, or compatible pointing device
Printer	Any Windows compatible printer

• If you intend to run Word Mail, you will need Microsoft Exchange Client or Microsoft Outlook.

Specification for Microsoft Office

If you are installing the whole of the Microsoft Office Professional suite, the above specification applies, with these amendments.

RAM	If you want to run 2 or more programs at once, you need at least 4Mb more RAM.
Hard Disk	Depending upon the edition and the choice of components, between 60 and 190 Mb.

───── 1.4 Installing Word 97 ─────

If you have bought a new computer at the same time as the software, the software is most probably pre-installed on your hard disk. If this is the case you can skip this bit.

As the general trend is towards buying office suites (rather than individual applications) you have probably purchased Microsoft Office in one of the three editions available:

- **Small Business** – Word, Excel, Publisher and Outlook
- **Standard** – Word, Excel, PowerPoint and Outlook
- **Professional** – as Standard, plus Access

The instructions below are for installing Microsoft Office under Windows 95 – if you've bought Word 97 on its own follow the instructions included with your CD or disk set.

1 Insert the Office CD in the CD-ROM drive, or if you're installing from floppy disks, insert the first Setup disk (Disk 1) in drive A or B
2 Click the **Start** button on the Taskbar
3 Choose **Settings**
4 Click **Control Panel**
5 Double-click the **Add/Remove Programs** icon
6 On the **Install/Uninstall** tab, click the Install button
7 Follow the Set up instructions on the screen

1.5 Starting Word 97

From the Start menu

1 Click the **Start** button on the Taskbar
2 Choose **Programs**
3 Click **Microsoft Word**

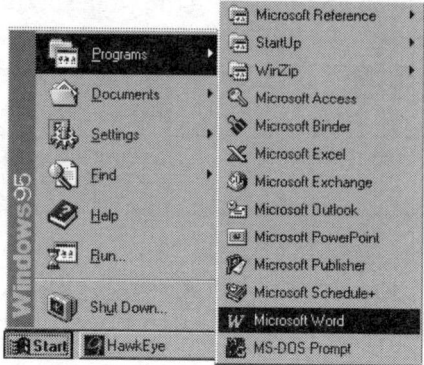

From the Shortcut Bar

1 Click the **Word** tool 🔟 on the Shortcut Bar
Or

2 Click the **New document** tool 🔳 on the Shortcut Bar
3 At the **New Document** dialog box, choose the General tab

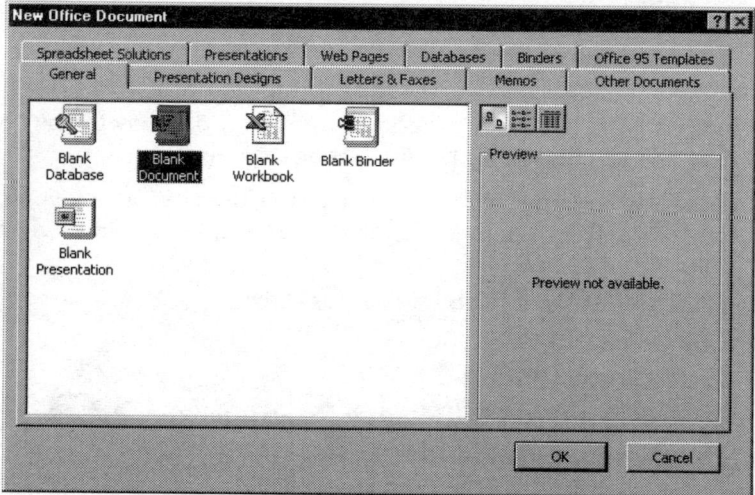

4 Select **Blank Document** and click **OK**

1.6 The Word screen

Whichever method you use to start Word, you are presented with a new blank document, so you can just start typing in your text.

We'll take a tour of the Word screen, so that you know what the various areas are called. You'll find the different screen areas referred to by their 'proper' names in the on-line help, throughout this book and in other publications on the package.

Application Title Bar

Document Title Bar

Menu Bar

Application Minimise, Maximise/Restore and Close

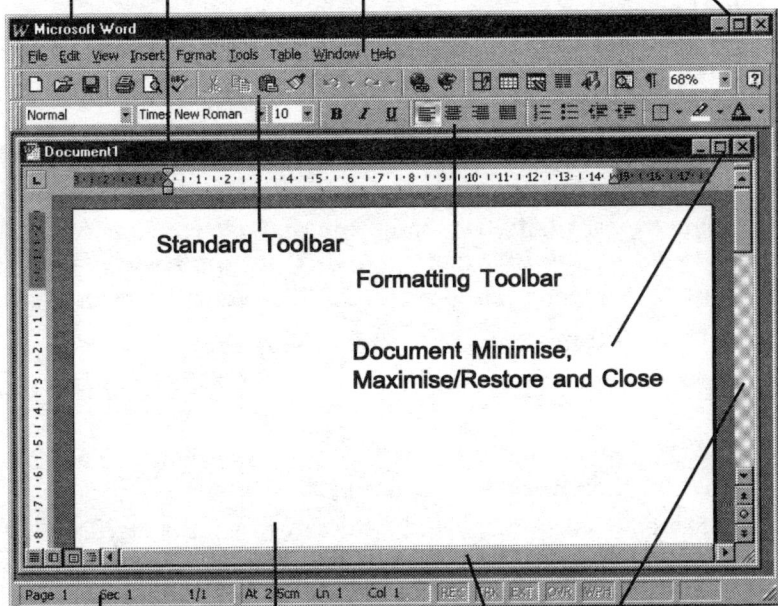

Standard Toolbar

Formatting Toolbar

Document Minimise, Maximise/Restore and Close

Status Bar   Document window   Horizontal and vertical scroll bars

If your Document window is maximised, the Document and the Application share one Title Bar containing the Application name and the Document name.

1.7 Menus

There are 9 main menus in your Word Application Window. You can use these menus to access any function or feature available in Word. I suggest you have a browse through them to get an idea of what's available – some menu items on the lists may appear familiar to you, some will be new.

You can display a <u>menu list</u> and select menu options using either the mouse or the keyboard.

USING THE MOUSE

1   Click on the menu name to display the list of options available in that menu
2   Click on the menu item you wish to use

USING THE KEYBOARD

Each menu name has one character underlined.

To open a menu:

•   Hold down the **[Alt]** key and press the underlined letter, e.g. **[Alt]-[F]** for the **File** menu, **[Alt]-[I]** for the **Insert** menu.

Each item in a menu list also has an underlined letter in it.

To select an item from the menu list either:

•   Press the appropriate letter.

    or

•   Use the up and down arrow keys until the item you want is selected, then press the **[Enter]** key.

Once a menu list is displayed, you can press the right or left arrow keys to move from one menu to another.

To close a menu without selecting an item from the list:

•   Click the menu name again, click anywhere off the menu list or press the **[Esc]** key on your keyboard.

In addition to the menus, many of the commands can be initiated using the toolbars, keyboard shortcuts or shortcut menus. Each of these areas will be covered as you progress through the book.

1.8 Help!

As you work with Word you will most probably find that you come a bit unstuck from time to time and need help! There are several ways of getting help – most of them very intuitive and user friendly.

Office Assistant

One of the first things you'll notice when working with any of the Office 97 applications is the Office Assistant. The Office Assistant replaces the Answer Wizard found in Office 95. It displays Help topics and tips through its 'dialog bubble', rather than a standard dialog box!

To call on the Office Assistant, press **[F1]** or click the Office Assistant tool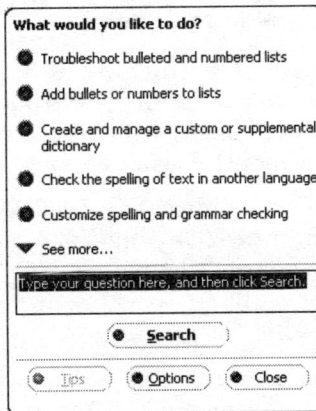

The Office Assistant will rush to your aid!

Depending on what you have been doing, the Assistant may display a list of topics that you might be interested in.

To choose a topic from the *'What would you like to do?'* list, simply click on the topic.

If you have a specific question you want to ask, type it in at the prompt and click the **Search** button.

The Assistant will display the Help page.

What would you like to do?

- Troubleshoot bulleted and numbered lists
- Add bullets or numbers to lists
- Create and manage a custom or supplemental dictionary
- Check the spelling of text in another language
- Customize spelling and grammar checking
- ▼ See more...

Type your question here, and then click Search.

Search

Tips   Options   Close

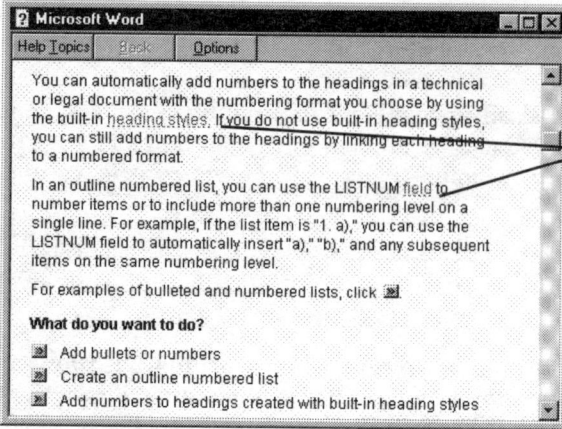

You can automatically add numbers to the headings in a technical or legal document with the numbering format you choose by using the built-in heading styles. If you do not use built-in heading styles, you can still add numbers to the headings by linking each heading to a numbered format.

In an outline numbered list, you can use the LISTNUM field to number items or to include more than one numbering level on a single line. For example, if the list item is "1. a)," you can use the LISTNUM field to automatically insert "a)," "b)," and any subsequent items on the same numbering level.

For examples of bulleted and numbered lists, click 🔳

What do you want to do?

🔳 Add bullets or numbers

🔳 Create an outline numbered list

🔳 Add numbers to headings created with built-in heading styles

If a word has a dotted underline, you can click on it for a short explanation

Some Help pages contain green words or phrases with a dotted green underline – these are technical terms or jargon that may be unfamiliar to you. To find out what the word or phrase means, point to it with the mouse and click.

Any related Help pages will be cross-referenced at the end of the Help page – to display a related page click on its cross-reference.

When you've finished exploring the Help system, click the Close button at the top right of the Help window.

The Office Assistant window can be left open as you work on your document, or you can close it and call on it as required. If you opt to leave it open, drag it (using its title bar) to an area of your screen where it doesn't obscure your work.

- If you leave the Office Assistant window open, click on it any time you want to ask a question.
- To close the Office Assistant window, click its Close button.

TO CUSTOMISE THE OFFICE ASSISTANT

You can customise the Office Assistant to take on a different appearance, or behave in a different way.

1 Open the Office Assistant

2 Click the **Options** button

3   To change its appearance, select the **Gallery** tab and browse through the options available (use the **Next** and **Back** buttons to move through the various guises)

•   If you find an Assistant you would like to use, click **OK**.

•   To leave the Assistant as it was, click **Cancel**.

4   To change its behavior, select the **Options** tab, select or deselect the options available – click on an option to switch it on or off. A tick in a box means an option is selected, an empty box means it isn't.

5   Click **OK** to set the options selected or **Cancel** to leave things as they were.

TIPS

The Office Assistant is constantly monitoring your actions. If it thinks that it has a tip that may be useful to you, a light bulb will light up in its window. To read its tip, click the bulb in the Office Assistant window.

If the Tips button is active in the Office Assistant dialog bubble, you can click it and then view the list of tips on offer (use the Next and Back buttons to move through them).

What's This?

If you haven't used Microsoft Office products before, or if you're new to the Windows environment, there will be many tools, menus, buttons and areas on your screen that puzzle you. The *What's This?* option works best when a document is open as most of the tools, menus and screen areas are active.

To find out what a tool does:

1   Hold down the **[Shift]** key and press **[F1]**. The mouse pointer looks like this ▶?

2   Click the tool

To find out about an item in a menu list:

1   Hold down the **[Shift]** key and press **[F1]**

2   Open the menu and select the option required from the list

To find out about anything else within the Word window:

1 Hold down the **[Shift]** key and press **[F1]**
2 Click on the item

If you accidentally invoke the *What's This* Help option, press **[Shift]-[F1]** (or the **[Esc]** key) to cancel it.

Contents and Index

You can also access the Help system from the Help menu. Use the Contents, Index or Find tabs to locate the Help pages you need. To get help through the Help menu:

1 Open the **Help** menu
2 Choose **Contents and Index**
3 At the **Help Topics** dialog box, select a tab from which to work – **Contents**, **Index** or **Find**

CONTENTS TAB

You can browse through the Help system from the Contents tab.

• Double click on a book to display or hide its list of contents.

Depending on the book you select, you may be presented with more books, a list of topics, or a mixture of both.

To display a topic:
1 Double click on it
2 Work through the system until you find the Help you need

To print a topic:
1 Select the topic on the **Contents** tab
2 Click **Print...**

or
1 Display the topic – double click on it
2 Click the **Options** button
3 Choose **Print Topic**

• Close the Help window when you're finished.

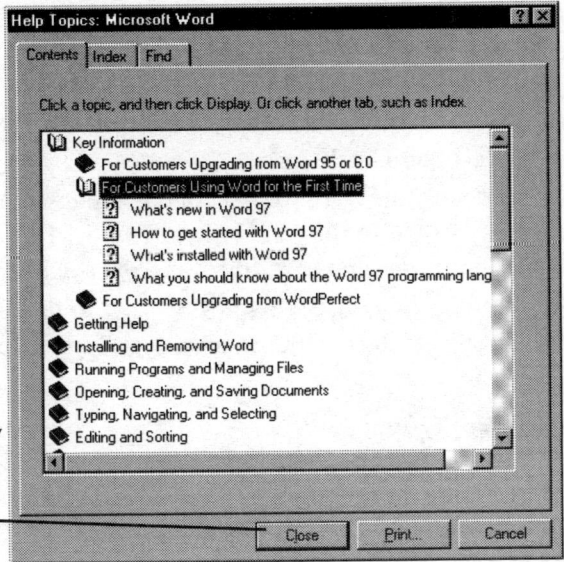

The button will show 'Close', 'Open' or 'Display', depending on what has been selected

INDEX TAB

If you know what you are looking for, the Index tab gives you quick access to any topic and is particularly useful once you are familiar with the terminology used in Word.

1 Choose **Contents and Index** from the Help menu
2 At the **Help Topics** dialog box, select the **Index** tab
3 Start typing in the word you're looking for
4 When the index entry appears in the list, select it
5 Click **Display**
6 A list of related topics or the Help Text requested will appear (depending on what you have selected from the index)
7 Continue until you find the Help you need
8 Close the Help window when you've finished

FIND TAB

The Find tab is used to search out specific words and phrases, rather than look for a particular category of information.

The first time you use the Find tab the *Find Setup Wizard* runs to set up your word list – just follow the prompts to set up your list (this only happens once).

1 Choose **Contents and Index** from the Help menu
2 Select the **Find** tab
3 Type in your word (or part of it – enough to get some matching words displayed)
4 Select a matching word to narrow the search
5 Double click on the topic you wish to display
6 Close the Help window when you're finished.

ScreenTips

If you point to any tool on a displayed toolbar, a ScreenTip will probably appear to describe the purpose of the tool.

If no ScreenTips appear, you can easily switch them on if you want to.

If you like using keyboard shortcuts, you may find it useful to customise the basic ScreenTip, so that it displays the keyboard shortcut for a command as well. This might help you learn the keyboard shortcuts more quickly.

To switch ScreenTips on or off or to turn on the keyboard shortcuts in ScreenTips:

1 Point to any toolbar and click the right mouse button
2 Choose **Customize...** from the shortcut menu
3 In the **Customize** dialog box select the **Options** tab
4 Select or deselect the **Show ScreenTips on toolbars** checkbox to turn the option on or off as required
5 Select the **Show shortcut keys in ScreenTips** option to have the keyboard shortcut for each tool displayed in the ScreenTip
6 Click **Close**

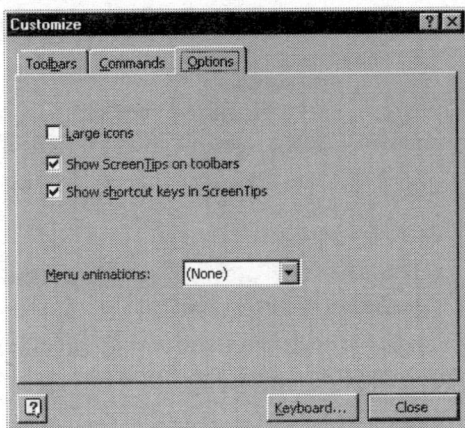

Dialog box Help

When you access a dialog box in Word, e.g. the Customize one above, you can get Help on any item within it that you don't understand. To get Help on an item in a dialog box:

1 Click the Help button [?] at the top right of the title bar
2 Click on an option, button or item in the dialog box that you want explained
• A brief explanation of the option, button or item you click on will be displayed.
3 Click anywhere within the dialog box to close the explanation.

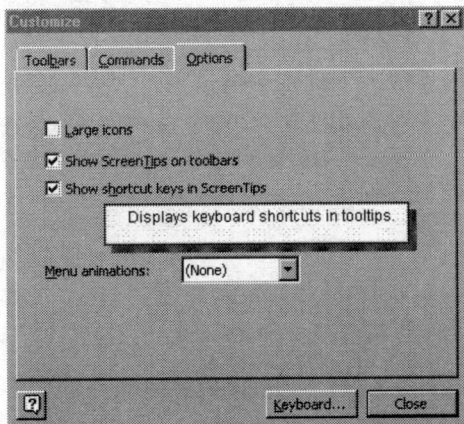

─────── 1.9 Exiting Word 97 ───────

When you have finished working in Word you must close the
application down – don't just switch off your computer!

1 Open the **File** menu and choose **Exit**

or

2 Click the **Close** button ☒ in the top right corner of the
   Application Title Bar

If you have edited a document, but have not saved it, you will be
prompted to do so – see *Save and Save As* in Chapter 2.

─────── 1.10 Summary ───────

In this chapter we have discussed:

* The fact that Word is a very powerful, yet easy to use, word
  processing package.
* The minimum software and hardware requirements necessary
  to run the package successfully.
* The installation procedure for the software.
* Accessing the package through the Start menu and the
  Shortcut Bar.
* The Word screen.
* Utilising the menu system using the mouse and the keyboard.
* The Office Assistant and On-line Help system.
* Exiting Word.

2

BASIC WORD SKILLS

2.1 Aims of this chapter

In this chapter we will discuss the basic skills you will need to acquire. By the time you have completed this chapter, you will know how to create, save, print, open and close documents. Spelling and grammar checking together with simple editing techniques for inserting, deleting, copying and moving text are covered, as are some options for viewing your document on screen.

2.2 Your first document

When you start Word, a new document is created automatically – all that you need to do is type in your text. The document name, *Document1*, is displayed on the document title bar.

Each new document you create during a session in Word is given a temporary name. Your second document will be called *Document2*, the next one *Document3* and so on. These names should be considered temporary – you will eventually save your document and give it a meaningful name instead of the temporary name assigned by Word.

Each time you access Word a new document, *Document1*, is displayed ready for you to enter your text.

The insertion point – the flashing black vertical bar – is in the top left of the text area on the first page. Just type. Your text will appear at the insertion point.

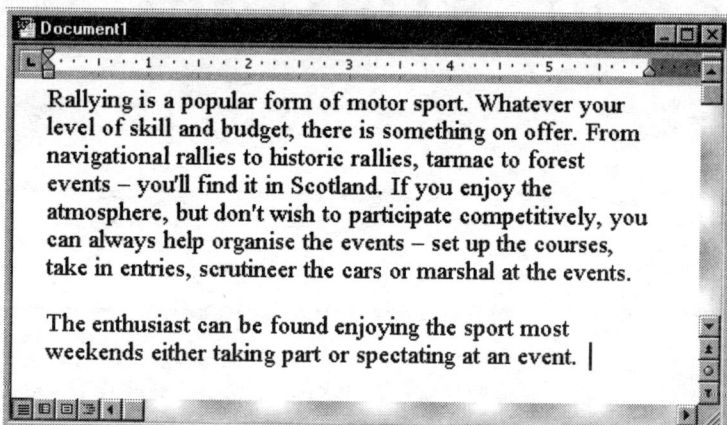

Things to remember when entering text into your document:

- DO NOT press the **[Enter]** key at the end of each line of text. If a sentence is going to run onto a new line, let it – the text will be wrapped automatically at the end of the line.

- DO press the **[Enter]** key at the end of short lines of text, e.g. after lines in the inside address (the name and address of the person you're sending the letter to) at the top of a letter or after the last line in a paragraph.

- To leave a clear line between paragraphs, or empty lines between headings or in the signature block at the end of a letter, keep pressing **[Enter]** until you get the effect you want.

2.3 Spelling and grammar

To help you produce accurate work, Word can check the spelling and grammar in your document. You can let Word either:

- Check your spelling and grammar as you work, and draw attention to any errors you make, as you make them

or

- You can check the spelling and grammar in your document when you are ready, and correct any errors at that stage.

Checking spelling and grammar as you work

This option is operational by default – if it doesn't work on your system, someone has switched it off.

- As you enter your text, any words that Word thinks are incorrectly spelt will be underlined with a red, wavy line.
- Any words, phrases or sentences that have unusual capitalisation or aren't grammatically correct will have a grey wavy underline.

To find out what Word thinks you should have done, right click (click the right mouse button) on the highlighted word or phrase and respond to the suggestions as appropriate.

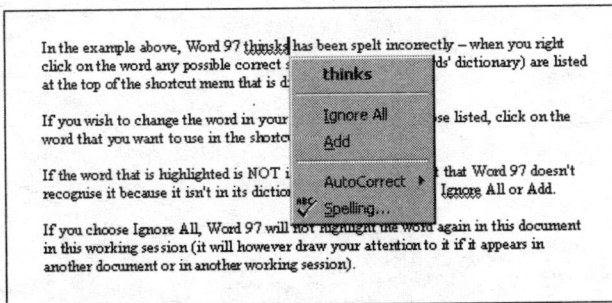

In the example above, 'thinks' has been spelt incorrectly – when you right click on the word any possible correct spellings (found in Word's dictionary) are listed at the top of the shortcut menu.

- If you wish to change the word to one of those listed, click on the word that you want to use in the shortcut menu.
- If the word that is underlined is correctly spelt, it's just that Word doesn't recognise the word because it isn't in its dictionary. You can choose to **Ignore All** or **Add**.
- If you choose **Ignore All**, Word will not highlight the word again in this document in this working session (it will however draw your attention to the word if it appears in another document or in another working session).
- If you choose **Add**, the word will be added to Word's dictionary, and recognised as a correctly spelt word from then on.

Grammatical errors can be dealt with in a similar way. When you right click on the error, Word will display the problem, and suggest a remedy if it can. You can choose whether you wish to change your text to that suggested or ignore any suggestion made.

Spell and Grammar Checker Options

The automatic spelling and grammar checks can be switched on or off to suit yourself.

Turn on the Ignore options, if appropriate, to save needless spelling checks

The choice of Writing style controls the rigour of the grammar checking

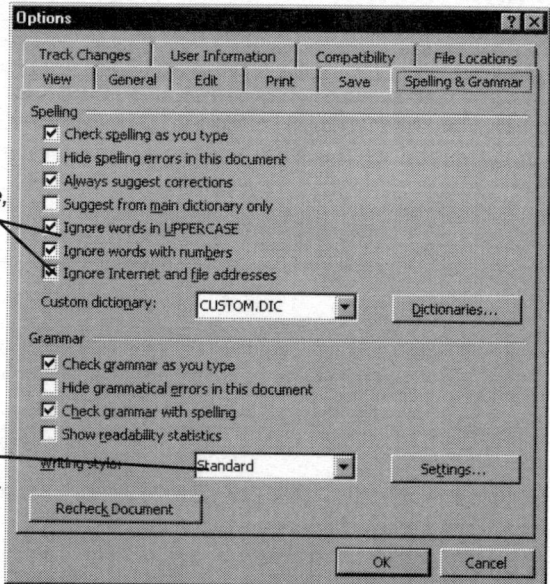

1 Open the **Tools** menu and choose **Options**
2 Open the **Spelling & Grammar** tab
3 Select or deselect the **Check spelling as you type** and **Check grammar as you type** options as required

Other spelling and grammar checking options are displayed in this dialog box. Come back to the **Options** dialog box and explore it using the on-line Help if your spell and grammar checkers are not acting as you would expect.

Checking spelling and grammar when you want to

You can easily check your spelling and grammar at any time using the Spelling and Grammar tool on the Standard toolbar.

1 Click the **Spelling and Grammar** tool 🔲

Word will check from the insertion point through to the end of your document. Respond to the prompts as you see fit. When the checking is complete, a prompt will appear to tell you so.

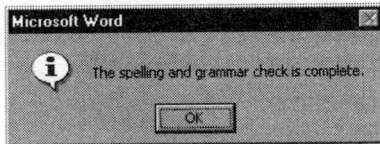

2 Click **OK** to return to your document

—— 2.4 Simple editing techniques ——

The spell and grammar checker will help you locate and fix some of your errors. It will not, however, correct everything.

You may decide to add some more text into the body of your document, or delete some that you no longer wish to use. You can add or delete as much text as you wish!

You can easily insert any characters that you have missed out, or delete any characters that you don't need.

Before you can insert or delete characters within existing text however, you must move the insertion point (the flashing vertical black bar) to the place where you want to edit.

Moving the insertion point

If the text you want to look at is not displayed on your screen, use the scroll bars to bring it into view.

There are many different ways to reposition the insertion point within your text – use the method which suits you.

USING THE MOUSE

1 Position the I-beam (the mouse pointer when it is over a text area) at the place you want to move the insertion point to

2 Click the left mouse button

USING THE KEYBOARD

To move a character or line at a time:

• Press the right, left, up or down arrow (cursor) keys until the insertion point is where you want it.

To move right or left a word at a time:

• Hold down [Ctrl] and press the right or left arrow key.

To move up or down a paragraph at a time:

• Hold down [Ctrl] and press the up or down arrow key.

Other useful ones are:

• Press [End] to move to the end of the line.
• Press [Home] to move to the beginning of the line.
• Press [Ctrl]-[Home] to move to the beginning of the document.
• Press [Ctrl]-[End] to move to the end of the document.

Experiment with the various options as you work.

Editing

TO INSERT NEW TEXT

1 Position the insertion point where you want the new text to appear – in the middle of a word (if you've missed out a letter or two).

2 Type in the new text.

TO DELETE EXISTING TEXT

1 Position the insertion point next to the character that you want to delete

2 If the insertion point is to the right of the character you want to delete, press the backspace key [←] once for each character.

   If the insertion point to the left of the character you want to delete, press the **[Delete]** key once for each character.

Both the [←] and **[Delete]** keys repeat – if you hold them down they will zoom through your text removing it much quicker than you could type it in, so be careful with them!

OVERTYPE

You can type over existing text, replacing old text with new in one operation, instead of deleting the old then entering the new.

*   To go into Overtype mode, double click the OVR button on the Status bar. When Overtype mode is on, OVR is shown in black.

Position the insertion point within some existing text and type – watch carefully to see what happens. The existing text will be replaced with the new text you enter.

*   To switch Overtype mode off, double click the OVR button again – the text on the button becomes dimmed.

2.5 Save and Save As

If you want to keep your file, you must save it. If you don't save your file it will be lost when you exit Word. You can save your file at any time – you don't have to wait until you've entered all your text and corrected all the errors. If you don't save your file, it may be lost if the computer crashes or there is a power failure. Try to get into the habit of saving your document regularly.

TO SAVE YOUR DOCUMENT

1 Click the **Save** tool ▢ on the Standard toolbar. The **Save As** dialog box will appear on your screen

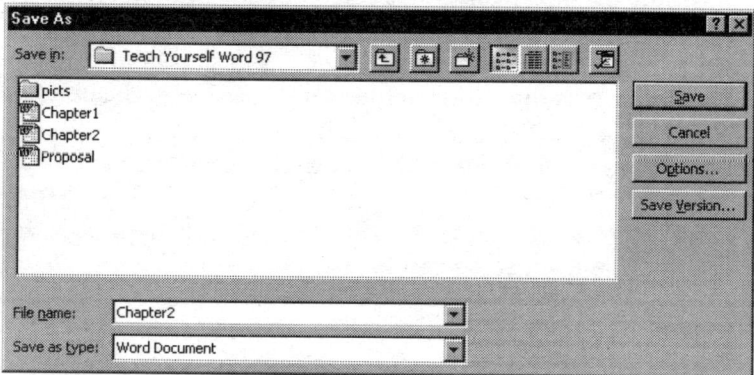

2 Specify the folder into which your file should be saved (the default is *My Documents*)
3 Give your file a name
4 Leave the **Save as type:** field at *Word Document*
5 Click **Save**

The name of your document will appear on the Document Title Bar in place of the temporary file name.

As your document develops, you can re-save your file any time you wish – just click the **Save** tool. The **Save As** dialog will not reappear, but the old version of the file on your disk will be replaced by the new, up-to-date version displayed on your screen.

SAVE AS

There may be times that you save a file, edit it, then decide that your want to save the edited file but also keep the original version of the file on disk.

If you don't want to overwrite the old file with the new version, save it using a different file name. You can save your file to the same folder, or you can select a different drive and/or folder.

1 Open the **File** menu and choose **Save As**

2 The **Save As** dialog will appear again

3 Enter a new name in the **File name** field

4 Click **Save**

- If you save the new version of the file into the same folder as the old one, you must use a different file name.

——— 2.6 Print Preview and Print ———

At some stage you will want to print your file. Before sending a document to print, it's a good idea to preview your document.

PRINT PREVIEW

The preview will display a full page of your document on the screen at once (more than one page if you wish) so that you can check how the finished page will look:

- How much space does your text take up?
- Is there a good balance of 'white space' (blank areas) and text?

If the preview looks good, you can send your document to the printer. If not, you might want to edit the layout to get a better-looking document.

- To preview your document, click the Print Preview tool

A full-page preview of your document will appear on screen.

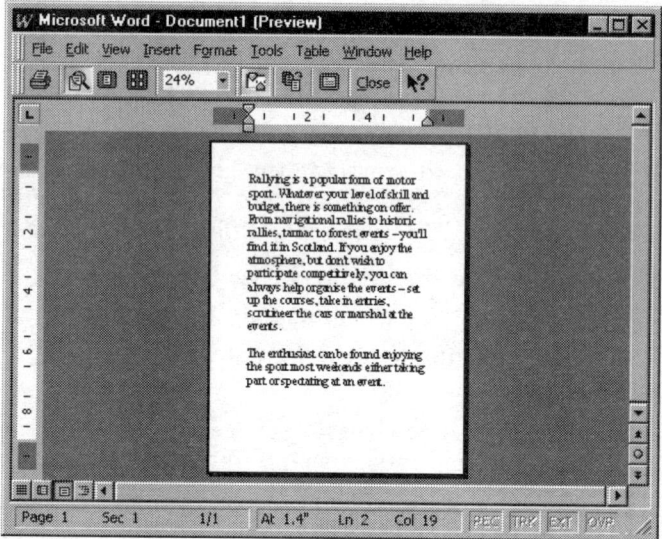

ZOOM

If you move your mouse pointer over your page in print preview, you will notice it looks like a magnifying glass with a **+** on it.

- Click the left mouse button and you will be zoomed in on your document so that you can read it.

When you are zoomed in, the magnifying glass has a **−** on it.

- Click to zoom out to get an overview of the page again.

EDITING TEXT IN PRINT PREVIEW

If you zoom in on your text, and notice something you want to change, you can edit the document when you are in print preview.

- Click the Magnifier tool 🔍 on the Print Preview toolbar.

The insertion point will appear in your document. You can use any editing techniques you wish on the text.

- To enable the zoom feature again, click the Magnifier tool.

PRINT

If you are happy with the appearance of your document, and

want to print it out from the preview window, click the Print
tool 🖨. One copy of your document will be sent to the printer.

Print Preview toolbar

The Print Preview window has its own toolbar which can be used
to control the display of your document on the screen.

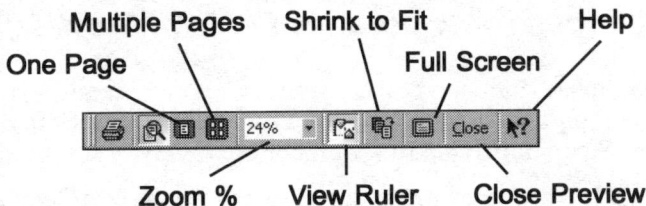

One Page
Click this tool to display one page on the screen at a time.

Multiple Pages
This tool drops down a grid that you can click and drag over to
indicate the number of pages you want to display at one time –
maximum number 6 across and 2 down.

Zoom %
This sets the percentage of magnification on your document.

View Ruler
Toggles the display of the vertical and horizontal rulers.

Shrink to Fit
If there is a small amount of text on the last page of your
document, you may be able to reduce the number of pages by
clicking this tool. Word decreases the size of each font used to
get the text to fit on to one page less. This feature works best
with relatively short documents – letters, memos, etc.

Full Screen
You can remove most of the toolbars, menu bar, title bar, etc, to
get a 'clean screen' display. To return the screen to normal, click
Close Full Screen on the Full Screen toolbar or press **[Esc]**.

Close Preview

Exits Print Preview and returns you to your document.

Context Sensitive Help

Click this tool, then click on a tool, scroll bar, ruler, etc, to get a brief description of its function. Once you've read the information, click anywhere on your screen to close the information box.

Moving through your document in Print Preview

If you have more than one page in your document, you may want to scroll through the pages in Print Preview to check that they look okay. You can do this in a number of ways:

- Click the arrow up or arrow down at the top or bottom of the vertical scroll bar.

- Press the **[PageUp]** or **[PageDown]** keys.

- Click the Previous Page or Next Page button at the bottom of the vertical scroll bar.

- Drag the scroll box up or down the vertical scroll bar until

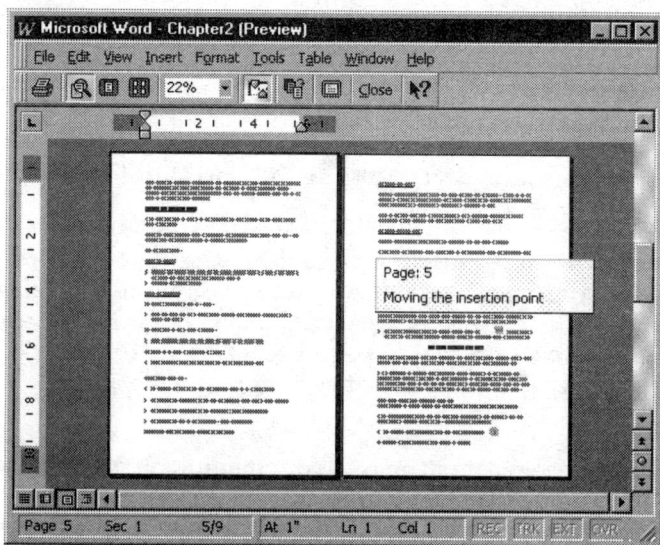

you reach the page you want to view (notice the prompt that tells you which page you've reached).

PRINT

To print one copy of the whole document:

- Click the Print tool 🖨 on either the Standard toolbar, or the Print Preview toolbar.

If you don't want to print the whole document, you can specify the pages you want printed in the Print dialog box.

1 Open the **File** menu and choose **Print** (or press **[Ctrl]-[P]**)

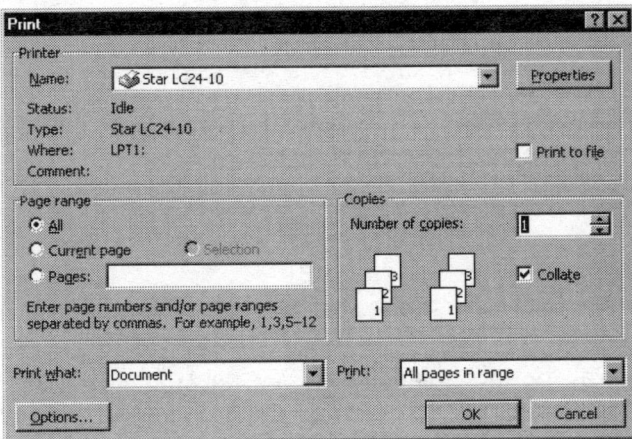

2 At the dialog box, specify the pages you want to print – **All**, **Current** (the one the insertion point is currently in) or **Pages**

- To print consecutive pages, enter the range in the **Pages** field in the format 5–12 (e.g. to print all the pages from 5 to 12).

- To print non-consecutive pages, enter the range in the format 5,7,12,30.

- To enter a mixture of consecutive and non-consecutive pages the format is 4,5,6–12,14.

3 Click **OK** once you've specified your page range

2.7 Close document

Once you've finished working on a document you should close it. You can have several documents open at the same time when working in Word and sometimes this is very useful. However, depending on how much memory your computer has, you may find that it slows down when you have several documents open. So, if you don't need to have a document open, close it.

To close your document:

• Open the **File** menu and choose **Close**.

or

• Click the **Close** button ⊠ at the top right of the document title bar.

You will be prompted to save the document if it has changed since the last time you saved it.

SHORTCUT MENU

As an alternative to using the toolbars or the menu bar to initiate commands, you may like to try the shortcut menu.

To display the shortcut menu click the right mouse button. The list of options displayed varies depending on where the insertion point is, or, on what you have selected.

2.8 Create a new blank document

It is very easy to create a new document when working in Word. The instructions here allow you to create a new document using the *blank document template*. A template is simply a pattern on which your document is based – every document you create in Word must take its pattern from a template.

The blank document template has an A4 size page, portrait orientation (tall ways up), with an inch margin at the top and bottom of the page, and an inch and a quarter margin at the left and right-hand side.

When you access Word, and are presented with the Document1 temporary file, that file is based on the blank document template.

To create a new document from the blank document template:

• Click the **New** tool ⬜ on the Standard toolbar.

A new document will appear on your screen, with a temporary file name such as *Document2* (the number in the name depends on how many documents you have created during the session).

— 2.9 Opening an existing document —

If you want to view, update or print a document that you have already created, saved and closed you must first open the document you want to work with.

To open an existing document:

1   Click the **Open** tool 📂 on the Standard toolbar
•   The **Open** dialog box will appear on your screen.
2   Locate the folder that your document is stored in (if necessary)
3   Select the document you wish to open – click on its name
4   Click **Open**

You can also open a document by double clicking on its name in the **Open** dialog box.

If the document you want to open is a recently used file (one of the last 4 you were working on) you will find its name displayed at the bottom of the **File** menu. You can open your document from here, rather than go through the Open dialog box.

1   Open the **File** menu
2   Click on the file name you want to open

─────2.10 Selection techniques─────

Selection techniques are very important in Word. You need to use them if you want to:

- Copy or move text within a document
- Copy or move text from one document to another
- Change the formatting of existing text
- Quickly delete large chunks of text

There are several ways to select text in Word – try some out and use whatever seems easiest for you.

Using the mouse

CLICK AND DRAG

1 Move the mouse pointer to one end of the block of text
2 Click and hold down the left mouse button
3 Keeping the mouse button held down, drag over the text until you have reached the other end of the text you want to select
4 Let go the mouse button

This method works well for relatively small chunks of text – where all the text you want to select is visible on the screen.

If you need to select a big chunk of text, click and drag can be very difficult to control – once your text starts to scroll things start to move very quickly and it can be difficult to see what is being selected.

CLICK – [SHIFT] – CLICK

This method is often easier to control than the click and drag method (especially if you are selecting a lot of text).

1 Click at one end of the text you want to select (this positions the insertion point at that point)
2 Move the mouse pointer (do not hold down the mouse button) to the other end of the text

3 Hold down the **[Shift]** key on your keyboard, and then click
   the left mouse button

All the text between the insertion point and the mouse pointer
should be selected. If it isn't, you most probably let go the **[Shift]**
key before you clicked – try again if this is the case!

Both the click and drag and the Click – [Shift] – Click methods
can be used to select any amount of text.

If you are selecting a standard unit of text – a word, a sentence,
a paragraph or the whole document – there are some special
selection techniques that you might like to try instead of those
described above.

A word	double click on it
A sentence	hold down the **[Ctrl]** key and click anywhere within the sentence
A paragraph	double click in the selection bar to the left of the paragraph you wish to select or triple click anywhere within the paragraph

The whole document triple click in the selection bar

TO DESELECT ANY UNIT OF TEXT:

* Click anywhere within your text, or press one of the arrow
  keys on your keyboard

Using the keyboard

If you prefer working with the keyboard rather than the mouse,
there are several selection techniques you can try. Selecting text
using the keyboard is really a variation on moving through your
document using the keyboard (discussed in 2.4 above).

Try these selection methods. All work from the insertion point.

To select a character or line at a time:
* Hold down **[Shift]** and press the right, left, up or down arrow
  (cursor) keys until you have selected the text required

To select right or left, a word at a time:

- Hold down the **[Shift]** and **[Ctrl]** keys and press the right or left arrow key until you have selected the text you need

To select up or down a paragraph at a time:

- Hold down the **[Shift]** and **[Ctrl]** keys and press the up or down arrow key until you have selected the required text

Other useful ones are:

- **[Shift]-[End]** to select to the end of the line
- **[Shift]-[Home]** to select to the beginning of the line
- **[Shift]-[Ctrl]-[Home]** to select to the beginning of the document
- **[Shift]-[Ctrl]-[End]** to select to the end of the document
- **[Ctrl]-[A]** to select the whole document

Experiment with the various options as you work.

2.11 Cut, Copy and Paste

When working on a document, you will sometimes find that you have entered the correct text but it's in the wrong place! It may be that it should be somewhere else in the document you are working on, or you might want it to go into another document.

You could delete the text and type it in again at the correct place, but it's much quicker (especially if it's more than a couple of words) to move or copy the text to its new location.

- If you want to remove the text from its current position, and place it somewhere else within your document you can move it from one place to another.

- If you want to keep the text, but repeat it in another place in the document (or in another document), you can copy it.

You can move or copy any amount of text – a word, several sentences or paragraphs, or a whole document! Before you can move or copy text you must select it (see 2.10 above).

Moving text (Cut and Paste)

1 Select the text you want to move

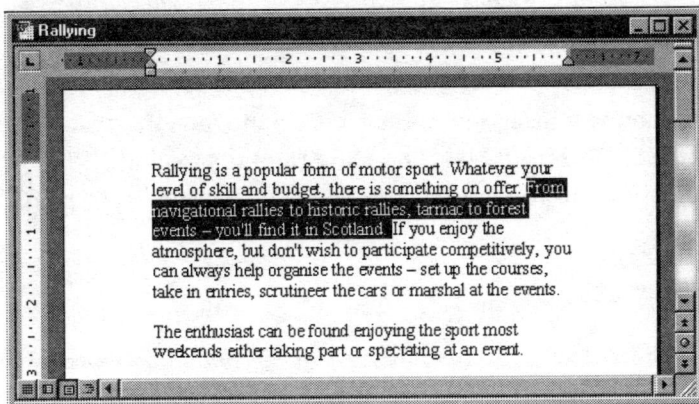

Rallying is a popular form of motor sport. Whatever your level of skill and budget, there is something on offer. From navigational rallies to historic rallies, tarmac to forest events – you'll find it in Scotland. If you enjoy the atmosphere, but don't wish to participate competitively, you can always help organise the events – set up the courses, take in entries, scrutineer the cars or marshal at the events.

The enthusiast can be found enjoying the sport most weekends either taking part or spectating at an event.

2 Click the **Cut** tool ✂ on the Standard toolbar
3 Position the insertion point where you want the text to go
4 Click the **Paste** tool 📋 on the Standard toolbar

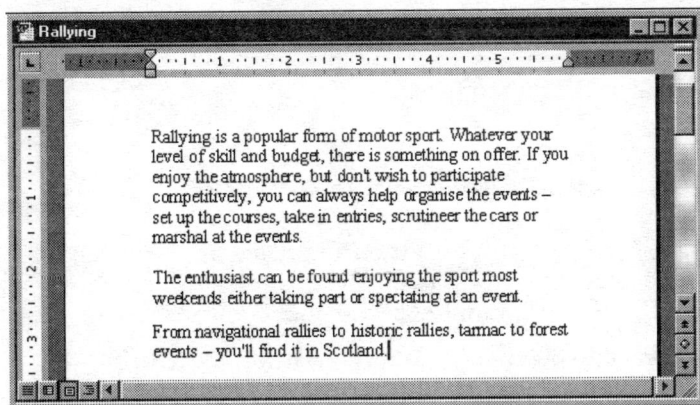

Rallying is a popular form of motor sport. Whatever your level of skill and budget, there is something on offer. If you enjoy the atmosphere, but don't wish to participate competitively, you can always help organise the events – set up the courses, take in entries, scrutineer the cars or marshal at the events.

The enthusiast can be found enjoying the sport most weekends either taking part or spectating at an event.

From navigational rallies to historic rallies, tarmac to forest events – you'll find it in Scotland.

The text will appear at the insertion point.

Copying text (Copy and Paste)

Copying text uses a similar technique, but the copied text remains in place, and a copy of it appears at the insertion point.

1 Select the text you want to copy
2 Click the **Copy** tool 🖺 on the Standard toolbar
3 Position the insertion point where you want the text to go
4 Click the **Paste** tool 🖺 on the Standard toolbar

A copy of the original text will appear at the insertion point.

The Clipboard

When you cut or copy text using the methods described above, the text that you cut or copy is placed in the *clipboard*. This is a temporary storage area that is used when you cut or copy. Anything you put in the clipboard remains there until you either cut or copy something else or until you exit Windows (it remains in the clipboard even if you close down the application).

If you cut or copy to the clipboard, then click the **Paste** tool, the clipboard contents will be pasted as often as you click **Paste**.

If you need more than one copy of something, copy it once and paste it as often as required.

Cut or Copy to a different document

You can move or copy text from one document to another. It's usually easier if you first open the document you want to move or copy the text from and also the one you want to paste into.

To go from one open document to another, use the **Window** menu – you will find a list of your open documents at the end of it.

The document currently displayed on screen is the one with a tick beside its name in the Window menu.

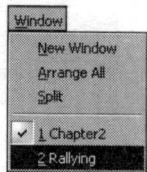

All the files listed in the Window menu are currently open – if you have a lot more listed than you anticipated, you are forgetting to close documents that you have finished working on.

To display another open document, open the Window menu and click on the name of the document you want to look at.

To move or copy text from one document to another:

1 Open the document you want to move or copy text from (the source document)

2 Open the document you want to move or copy the text to (the destination document)

3 Display the document you want to move or copy text from

4 Select the text you want to move or copy

5 Click the **Cut** ✀ or **Copy** tool 🗐 on the Standard toolbar

6 Display the document you want to move or copy the text to

7 Position the insertion point where you want the text to go

8 Click the **Paste** tool 📋 on the Standard toolbar

Your text will appear at the insertion point.

UNDO

If you accidentally make a mistake when you are working – don't panic! You can **undo** what you just did by clicking the Undo tool 🔙 on the Standard toolbar.

If the action you want to undo was not the last thing you did, click the drop-down arrow on the right to display a list of the actions you can undo. Scroll through the list until you find the action you want to undo and click on it. *When you undo an action from the list,* **all** *the actions above it are also undone.*

If you change your mind, click the Redo tool 🔜 to put things back as they were, or click the drop-down arrow to the right of the tool and select the action you want to redo from the list.

If the Redo tool is dimmed, there is nothing that can be redone!

2.12 Drag and drop

As an alternative to using Cut or Copy and Paste techniques to move and copy text, you may find *drag and drop* useful.

Drag and drop is especially useful when moving or copying a small amount of text a short distance – i.e. to somewhere else on the screen.

If you try to drag and drop text a long way, you will probably find that your text scrolls very quickly on the screen and that it is very difficult to control.

To MOVE

1 Select the text that you want to move or copy
2 Position the mouse pointer anywhere over the selected text
3 Click and hold down the left mouse button (notice the 'ghost' insertion point that appears within the selected text area)
4 Drag your mouse until the ghost insertion point is where you want your text moved to
5 Let go the mouse button

To COPY

Copying text is just like moving it, but this time you hold down the **[Ctrl]** key on your keyboard.

1 Select the text that you want to move or copy
2 Position the mouse pointer anywhere over the selected text
3 Hold down your **[Ctrl]** key
4 Click and hold down the left mouse button (notice the 'ghost' insertion point that appears within the selected text area)
5 Drag your mouse until the ghost insertion point is where you want your text moved to
6 Let go the mouse button
7 Let go the **[Ctrl]** key

—— 2.13 Normal vs Page Layout view ——

When working in a document, there are several viewing options available. The viewing option you select controls how your document looks on the screen – not how it will print out.

You will usually work in Normal view when entering your text, but Page Layout view is useful if you want to see where your text actually appears on the page.

Normal view

Normal view is the pre-set view for working in Word. It is the view usually used for entering, editing and formatting text.

The page layout is simplified in Normal View – margins, headers and footers, multiple columns, pictures, etc – are not displayed.

To change to Normal view:

1 Open the **View** menu
2 Choose **Normal**

or

1 Click the **Normal view** tool at the bottom left of the screen

Page Layout view

In this view you can see where your objects will be positioned on the page. Your margins are displayed (and any headers or footers you have within them), and pictures, drawings, multiple columns, etc, are all displayed in their true position on the page.

Page Layout view is useful if you are working with headers and footers, altering your margins, working in columns, or are combining text and graphics on a page and wish to see how they will be placed relative to each other.

In some chapters, Page Layout view will be recommended.

To change to Page Layout view:

1 Open the **View** menu
2 Choose **Page Layout**

or

1 Click the **Page Layout view** tool ▣ at the bottom left of the screen

———————— **2.14 Summary** ————————

In this chapter we have discussed some of the basic skills you require to use Word efficiently. You have learnt how to:

• Enter text.
• Spell check your document.
• Edit text.
• Move around your document using the mouse and the keyboard.
• Save your document.
• Print preview and print your file.
• Close a document.
• Create a new document.
• Open an existing document.
• Select text using the mouse and the keyboard.
• Move and copy text within a document.
• Move and copy text to another document.
• Move and copy text using drag and drop techniques.
• View your document using Normal view and Page Layout view.

3

FORMATTING TEXT

3.1 Aims of this chapter

In this chapter we will look at some of the ways you can enhance your text to help give your documents more visual impact. We will discuss the font and paragraph formatting options available.

3.2 Font formatting

One way of enhancing your text is to apply font formatting to it. The effects can be applied to individual characters in a document.

Unless you specify otherwise, each character is formatted to use the Times New Roman font (or typeface) with a size of 10 points.

Formatting can enhance your characters – underline them, increase their size, change colour, or make them bold or italic.

The most commonly used font formatting options have tools on the **Formatting** toolbar – other options can be found in the **Format, Font** dialog box.

Style   Font name   Font size   Bold   Italic   Underline

Alignment

Colour

Numbered list

Borders

Bulleted list   Indent level   Highlight

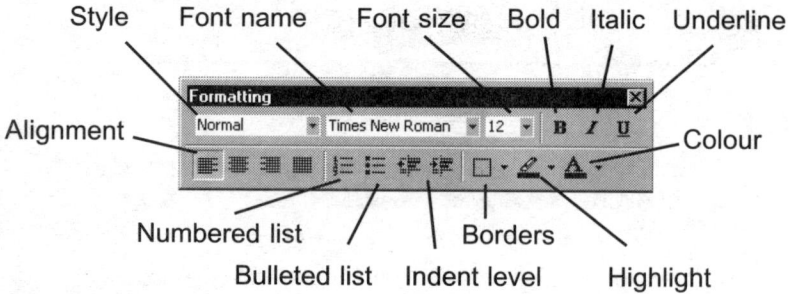

When applying font formatting you can either:

• Format text as it is entered.
or
• Enter your text and then apply the formatting to it.

_____ 3.3 Bold, italic and underline _____

The bold, italic and underline font formatting options are toggles – you switch them on and off in the same way. It is simplest to set them with the tools on the Formatting toolbar.

• To switch bold on or off, click the **Bold** tool **B**
• To switch italic on or off, click the *Italic* tool *I*
• To switch underline on or off, click the <u>Underline</u> tool <u>U</u>

To format text as you key it in:

1 Switch on the formatting option – bold, italic or underline
2 Enter your text
3 Switch the formatting option off when you reach the end of the text you want formatted

---

KEYBOARD SHORTCUTS

You can switch Bold, Italic and Underline on and off using the keyboard shortcuts **[Ctrl] - [B]**, **[Ctrl] - [I]** and **[Ctrl] -[U]**.

Rallying

Rallying is a popular form of motor sport. Whatever your level of skill and budget, there is something on offer. If you enjoy the atmosphere, but don't wish to participate competitively, you can always help organise the events – set up the courses, take in entries, scrutineer the cars or marshal at the events.

The enthusiast can be found enjoying the sport most weekends either taking part or spectating at an event.

From **navigational** rallies to **historic** rallies, **tarmac** to **forest** events – you'll find it in Scotland.

Contact *Jim McDonald* for more information.

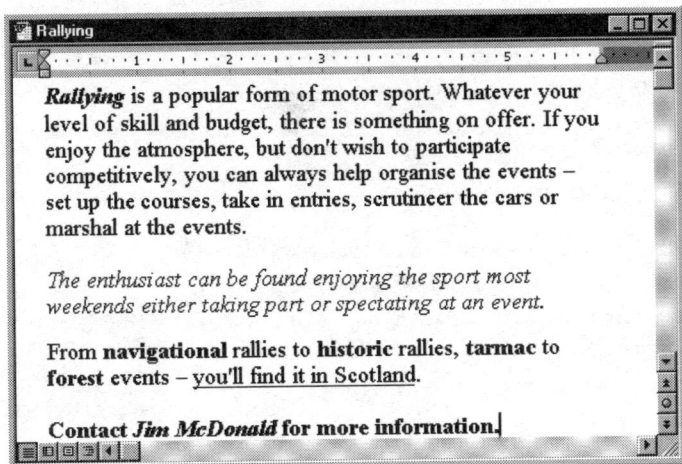

To format existing text:

1 Select the text you want to format (see 2.10)
2 Click the appropriate tool to apply the formatting required

To remove formatting from text:

1 Select the text
2 Click the **Bold**, **Italic** or **Underline** tool as necessary to remove the formatting

3.4 Font styles, size and colour

The font style, size and colour are also easily changed.

To change the style of font:

1 Click the drop-down arrow to the right of the **Font** tool on the Formatting toolbar
2 Scroll through the list of available fonts until you see the font you want to use
3 Click on it

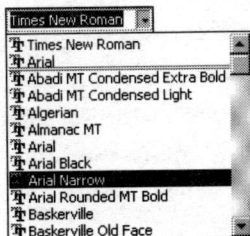

Times New Roman
Times New Roman
Arial
Abadi MT Condensed Extra Bold
Abadi MT Condensed Light
Algerian
Almanac MT
Arial
Arial Black
Arial Narrow
Arial Rounded MT Bold
Baskerville
Baskerville Old Face

To change the size of font:

1 Click the drop-down arrow to the right of the **Font Size** tool on the Formatting toolbar

2 Scroll through the list of available fonts until you see the size you want to use

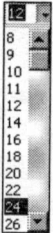

3 Click on it

To change the colour of font:

1 Click the drop-down arrow to the right of the **Font Color** tool on the Formatting toolbar to display the Font Color toolbar

2 Select the colour you want to use

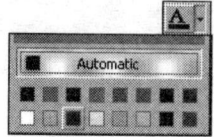

3.5 Highlight text

To highlight your text (the equivalent to using a marker pen on it) use the Highlight tool on the Formatting toolbar. The highlight you apply prints out – if you have a black and white printer, the colour will appear as grey shading behind your text.

To apply highlight to existing text:

1 Click the drop-down arrow to the right of the Highlight tool on the Formatting toolbar

2 Select the highlight colour you want to use

3 Click and drag over the text that you want to highlight (the mouse pointer looks like the I-beam with a marker pen attached!)

4 Click the Highlight tool again to switch the function off

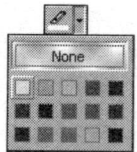

To remove highlight from existing text:

1 Select the text that has the highlight applied to it

2 Display the highlight options

3 Select **None**

AUTOMATIC SELECTION

If you wish to format an existing word, you do not need to
select it. Just position the insertion point anywhere inside the
the word, then apply the font formatting. Word automatically
formats the whole word surrounding the insertion point.

3.6 And yet more options

Explore the Font dialog box to find out what other font formatting
options are available. Try some out on your text.

1 Open the **Format** menu and choose **Font**
2 Select the tab – **Font**, **Character Spacing** or **Animation**
3 Choose the effects you want – a preview of your selection is
   displayed in the Preview window

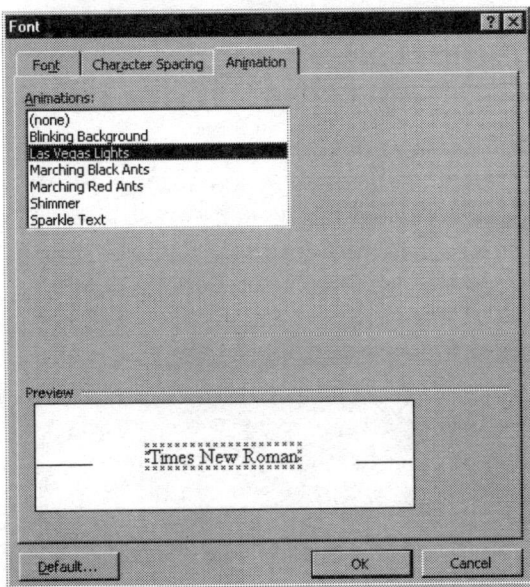

Animation really
makes headings
stand out – but use
this sparingly!

The Font panel has
many more options
than are on the
Formatting toolbar

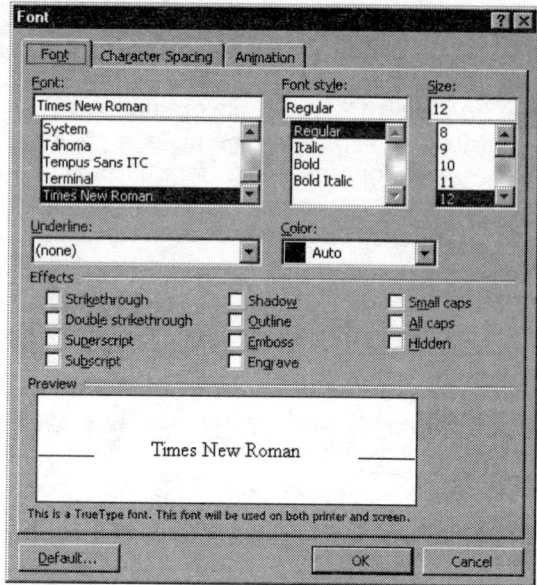

4 Click **OK** to apply the effects to your text, or **Cancel** to return
to your document without making any changes

DEFAULT FONT

The default font is the one that is used when you create a new
document – initially it is set to Times New Roman, size 10.

You can change these font options. Set the options you require
as your default using the tabs in the Font dialog box, and click
the **Default...** button. A dialog appears asking you to confirm
the change.

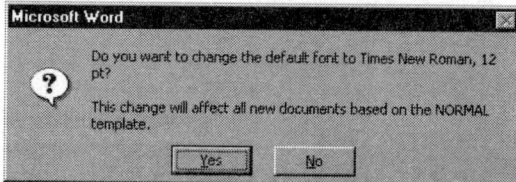

Click **Yes** to confirm, **No** if you've changed your mind.

3.7 Paragraph formatting

Some formatting options are applied to a complete paragraph, regardless of whether it consists of a few words or several lines. A paragraph is created in Word each time you press the **[Enter]** key. The heading at the top of this text is a paragraph, as is the empty line below it, and this is a paragraph. Each time you press the **[Enter]** key you insert a paragraph mark into your document.

Paragraph formatting options include:

- Alignment
- Borders and shading
- Numbered lists
- Tabs
- Line spacing
- Bulleted lists
- Indents

Show/Hide non-printing characters

You can toggle the display of the paragraph marks in your document using the Show/Hide tool ¶ on the Standard toolbar. The paragraph marks are non-printing characters – they do not print out even if they are displayed on your screen.

Other non-printing characters, e.g. a dot for each space you make by pressing the spacebar or an arrow to show that you have pressed the **[Tab]** key, are also displayed on your screen.

Specifying paragraph formatting

When applying paragraph formatting to text you can either:

- Format your paragraphs as they are entered.

or

- Enter your text and then go back and apply the paragraph formatting required later.

The default paragraph formatting options (the ones normally used) give you a left-aligned paragraph, with single line spacing. If this is not the formatting you require you can change it.

AUTOMATIC SELECTION

If you wish to apply formatting to an existing paragraph, you do not need to select the whole paragraph. Just position the insertion point anywhere inside it, then apply the paragraph formatting – Word automatically formats the paragraph surrounding the insertion point.

To change the paragraph formatting of consecutive existing paragraphs, select them first, and then change the formatting.

To format paragraphs as you enter text:

1 Select the paragraph formatting options required -alignment (see 3.8), line spacing (see 3.9), etc

2 Type in your text – each time you press the **[Enter]** key, the paragraph formatting options you have set will carry forward with you to the next paragraph

3 Press **[Enter]** at the end of the last paragraph that you want the formatting applied to

4 Select the next formatting option required

To format existing paragraphs:

1 Select the paragraph you want to format (see 2.10)

2 Specify the formatting required

DELETING PARAGRAPH MARKS

When you delete a paragraph mark, you delete the formatting codes that it holds. The paragraph then picks up its formatting from the next paragraph mark. If the paragraph formatting in the next paragraph mark is different you will notice the appearance of your paragraph change.

It is a good idea to work with the paragraph marks showing so that you don't accidentally delete one.

3.8 Alignment

The alignment of your paragraphs can be left, right, centre or justified. The default alignment is left, where the text is flush with the left margin and has a ragged right-hand edge.

This example shows centred, justified, right and left alignments.

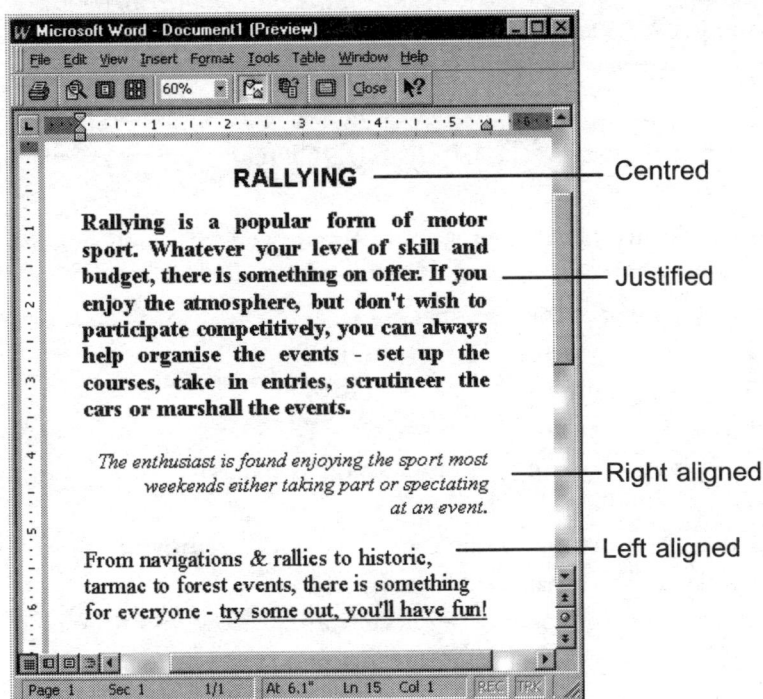

To centre a paragraph (or paragraphs):

• Click the Centre tool ▤ on the Formatting toolbar

To justify a paragraph (or paragraphs):

• Click the Justify tool ▦ on the Formatting toolbar

To right align a paragraph (or paragraphs):

• Click the Align Right tool ▦ on the Formatting toolbar

To left align a paragraph (or paragraphs):

• Click the Align Left tool 🔲 on the Formatting toolbar

KEYBOARD SHORTCUTS

You can specify the alignment using keyboard shortcuts:
[Ctrl]-[L] for left align, **[Ctrl]- [R]** for right align, **[Ctrl]-[E]** for centre and **[Ctrl]- [J]** for Justify.

——— 3.9 Line spacing ———

Initially, your line spacing is set to single. You can easily change to double or 1½ line spacing if you wish.

You can easily set the line spacing with the keyboard shortcuts:

• Double line spacing   **[Ctrl]-[2]**
• 1½ line spacing   **[Ctrl]-[5]**
• Single line spacing   **[Ctrl]-[1]**

Alternatively, you can open the **Paragraph** dialog box and select a line spacing option from there.

1 Open the **Format** menu and choose **Paragraph**
2 Select the **Indents and Spacing** tab
3 Choose the line spacing required from the **Line spacing:** field
4 Click **OK**

Line spacing options

Single	Accommodates the largest font in the line, and adds some extra space – how much depends upon the font
1½	1½ times that of single
Double	Double that of single
At Least	Minimum – Word can adjust to accommodate larger font sizes and graphics. Set the value in the **At:** field.

Exactly	Fixed line spacing. Set the value in the **At:** field.
Multiple	Increased or decreased by a fraction. e.g. 1.5 would increase the spacing by 50% (the same as 1½ line spacing) 1.8 would increase the spacing by 80%. The default is 3. Set the value in the **At:** field.

———— 3.10 Borders and shading ————

Borders and shading are also paragraph formatting options that can be very useful for emphasising areas in your document.

To place a border around a paragraph or paragraphs:

1 Select the paragraph or paragraphs
2 Click the drop-down arrow to the right of the **Borders** tool to display the **Borders** toolbar
3 Select a border from the options available

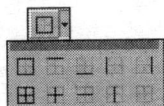

To remove a border from your paragraph or paragraphs:

1 Select the paragraph or paragraphs
2 Display the **Borders** toolbar
3 Click the **No Border** tool at the bottom right

There are more options in the **Borders and Shading** dialog box. You can apply a border to all 4 sides (an outside border) using the Box, Shadow or 3-D setting.

1 Open the **Format** menu and choose **Borders and Shading...**
2 Select the **Borders** tab
3 Choose a **Setting** from the list – **Box**, **Shadow** or **3-D**
4 Pick a line style from the **Style** list
5 Select the **Colour** and the line **Width** required
6 Click **OK**

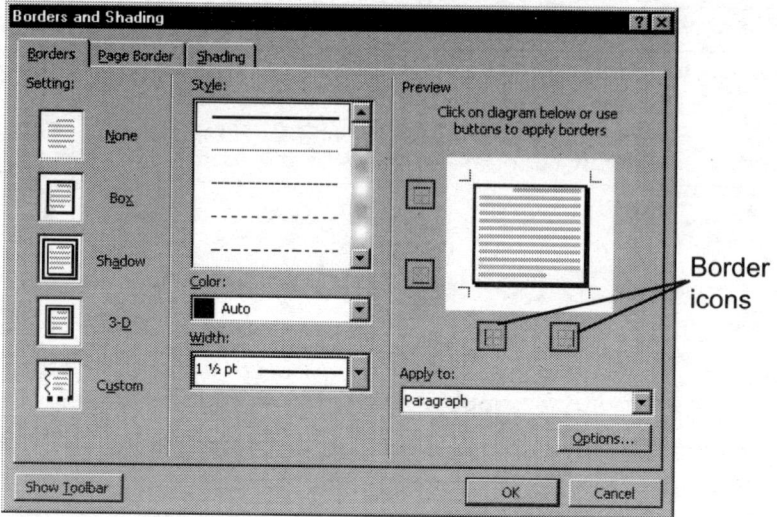

Border
icons

To switch individual borders (left, right, top or bottom) on and
off, click the border icons in the Preview window, or the lines
around the edges of the example in the Preview window.

If you choose **Custom** border from the **Setting** list, you can
specify different borders for different sides of the selected area.

1   Open the **Format** menu and choose **Borders and Shading...**
2   Select the **Borders** tab
3   Choose the **Custom** setting from the list on the left
4   Pick a line style from the **Style** list
5   Select the **Colour** and the line **Width** required
6   Click on the appropriate icon or line in the Preview window
7   Repeat steps 4 to 6 until you've specified all the borders
8   Click **OK**

To shade your paragraph or paragraphs, use the Shading
tab in the Borders and Shading dialog box.

1   Select the paragraph or paragraphs you want to shade
2   Open the **Format** menu and choose **Borders and Shading...**
3   Select the **Shading** tab

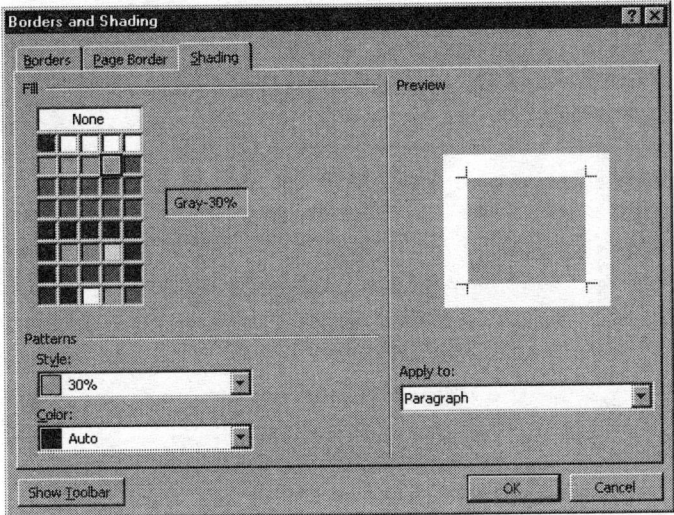

4 Choose a **Fill** colour
5 Pick a **Style** and **Colour** if you wish
6 Click **OK**

BLACK and WHITE

The higher the percentage of the grey fill colour, the harder it gets to read your text (unless you change your font colour). However, if you choose Black, or a grey fill colour of 80% or more, Word automatically displays the text as white.

The text in the example on the next page has a top and bottom border on the heading, black shading on the middle paragraph, and an outside border around the last paragraph.

```
W Microsoft Word - RALLYING.doc (Preview)                    _ □ ✕
File  Edit  View  Insert  Format  Tools  Table  Window  Help
🖨  🔍 ▣ ▦  60%  ▾  🖳  🗃  ▢  Close  ▖?
L  · · ·1· · · X· · · I · · ·1· · · I · · ·2· · · I · · ·3· · · I · · ·4· · · I · · ·5· · ·▲ · · ·6· · · ·
```

RALLYING

**Rallying is a popular form of motor
sport. Whatever your level of skill and
budget, there is something on offer. If you
enjoy the atmosphere, but don't wish to
participate competitively, you can always
help organise the events - set up the
courses, take in entries, scrutineer the
cars or marshall the events.**

*The enthusiast is found enjoying the sport most
weekends either taking part or spectating at an
event.*

From navigations & rallies to historic,
tarmac to forest events, there is something
for everyone - <u>try some out, you'll have fun!</u>

Contact Jane McDonald for more information

```
Page 1   Sec 1      1/1    At 7.9"   Ln 20  Col 26    REC  TRK  EXT  OVR  WPH
```

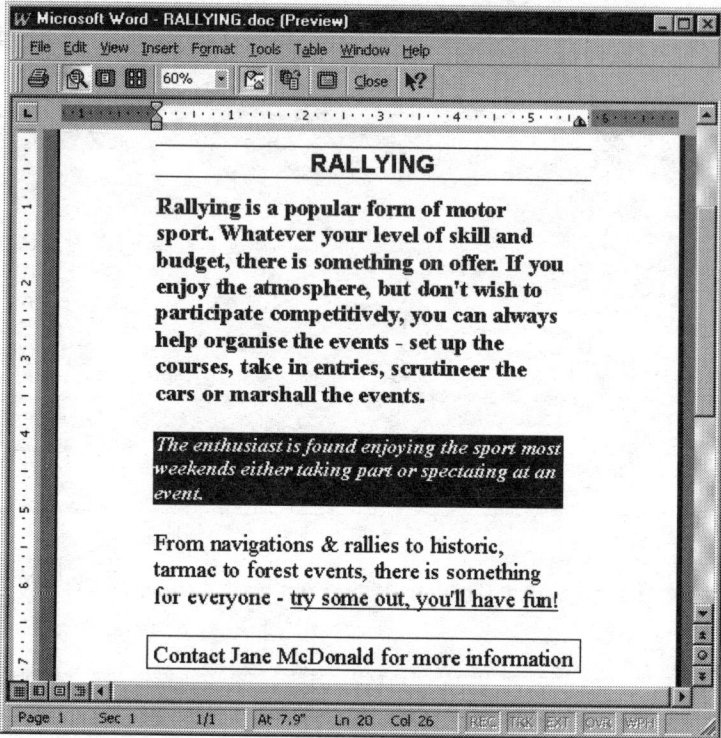

3.11 Bulleted lists

You can easily add bullets automatically to your paragraphs.

To add bullets as you enter your text:

1 Click the **Bullets** tool ▤ on the Formatting toolbar
2 Type in your text
3 Press the **[Enter]** key to create a new paragraph – it is
automatically given a bullet
4 Press the **[Enter]** key twice, without entering any text, and
the bullets are switched off

To add bullets to existing paragraphs:

1 Select the paragraphs
2 Click the **Bullets** tool

To remove bullets from existing paragraphs:

1 Select the paragraphs
2 Click the **Bullets** tool

To change the bullet style:

1 Select the paragraphs you want bulleted
2 Open the **Format** menu and choose **Bullets and Numbering**
3 Select the **Bulleted** tab in the dialog box
4 Choose a bullet
5 Click **OK**

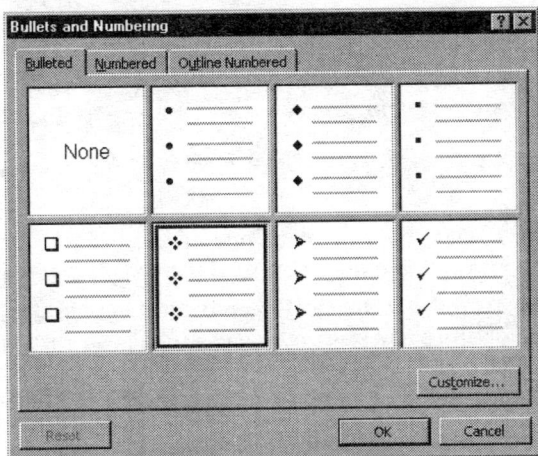

NUMBERED LISTS

You can number your paragraphs in much the same way as you apply bullets to them – just use the Numbering tool ⊞. Word keeps your numbering up to date as you edit your list. If you add extra paragraphs into your list, delete some, move or copy them, Word will automatically renumber the list.

Customized bullets

1 Select the paragraphs you want bulleted
2 Open the **Format** menu and choose **Bullets and Numbering**
3 Select the **Bulleted** tab in the dialog box
4 Choose a bullet from those displayed
5 Click the **Customize** button

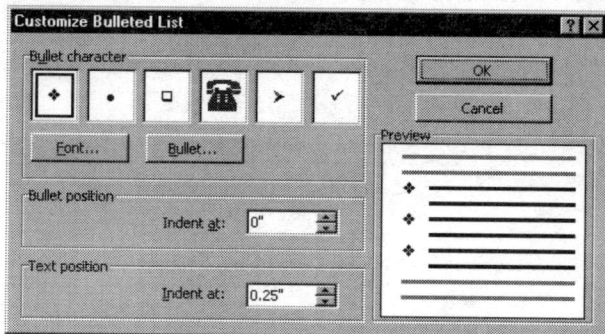

- To set the size or colour of the bullet, click the **Font** button, change the settings in the Font dialog box and click **OK**.
- To get a new bullet character, click the **Bullet** button and explore the character sets until you find a character you want to use. Change the character set through the **Font** list in this dialog box, and select a character by clicking on it.

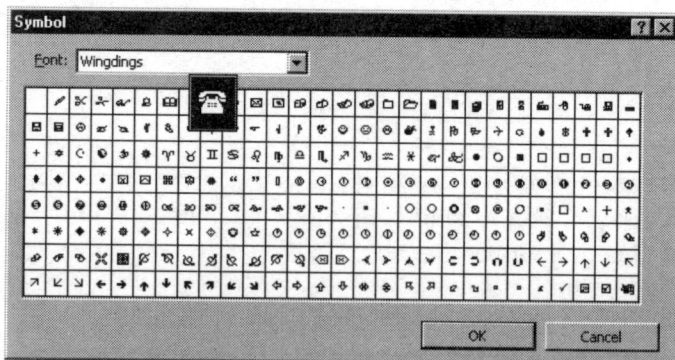

6   Click **OK** to confirm your changes in the Font or Symbol dialog box

7   Click **OK** to confirm your choice in the **Customize Bulleted List** dialog box

------------------------------ **3.12 Indents** ------------------------------

Your paragraphs normally run the full width of your typing line – from the left margin to the right margin. As you enter your text, it extends along the line until it reaches the right margin and then it automatically wraps to the next line (unless you press the **[Enter]** key.

In fact your text actually runs from the left indent marker to the right indent marker (not from left to right margin) – the left and right indent markers are flush with the left and right margins unless you set them differently.

If you want to leave some white space between your text and the margin you can move the indent markers to another position. Paragraphs that do not have text running from margin to margin are indented paragraphs.

You can change the position of the indents in the Paragraph dialog box, or you can drag the indent markers to the required position on the ruler (see page 57).

To change the indents using the Paragraph dialog box:

1   Open the **Format** menu and choose **Paragraph**

2   Select the **Indents and Spacing** tab

3   Set the left and/or right indent required in the **Left** and **Right** fields in the **Indentation** area of the dialog box – this will be applied to all the lines in your paragraph

4   Special indent effects – **Hanging** or **First line** only – can be specified in the **Special** list field

5   Watch the Preview window to see the effect you are creating

6   Click **OK** to confirm your settings

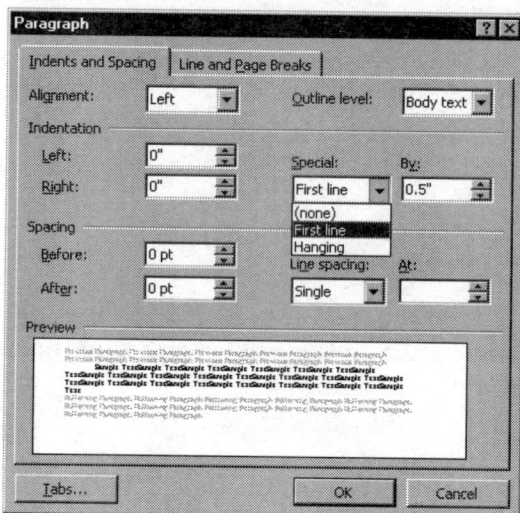

Some of the effects are illustrated below.

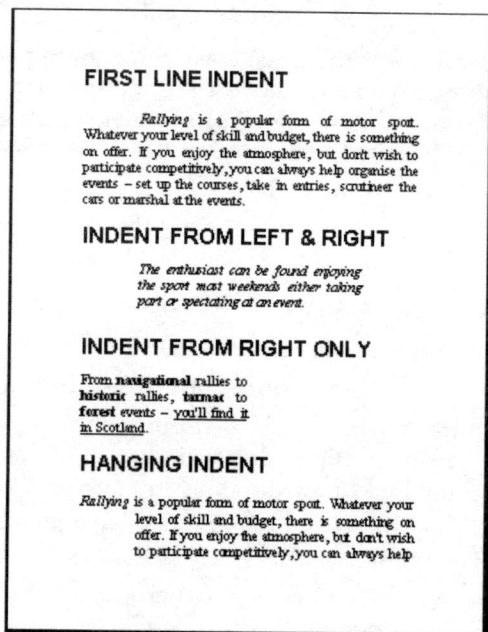

FIRST LINE INDENT

Rallying is a popular form of motor sport. Whatever your level of skill and budget, there is something on offer. If you enjoy the atmosphere, but don't wish to participate competitively, you can always help organise the events – set up the courses, take in entries, scrutineer the cars or marshal at the events.

INDENT FROM LEFT & RIGHT

The enthusiast can be found enjoying the sport most weekends either taking part or spectating at an event.

INDENT FROM RIGHT ONLY

From **navigational** rallies to **historic** rallies, **tarmac** to **forest** events – you'll find it in Scotland.

HANGING INDENT

Rallying is a popular form of motor sport. Whatever your level of skill and budget, there is something on offer. If you enjoy the atmosphere, but don't wish to participate competitively, you can always help

INDENTS MAKE LIFE EASY

Don't be tempted to push your text along each line in your paragraph using spaces or tabs – or cut each line in your paragraph short by pressing the [Enter] key – to get an indented effect. It can result in a lot of extra work and unnecessary frustration if you need to go back and insert or delete text later.

Changing the indents using the ruler

You can also use the ruler to set your indents. The ruler must be displayed along the top of your text area – if it's not, open the **View** menu and choose **Ruler** to display it.

The indent markers are the two triangles and the small rectangle below them at the left of the ruler, and the triangle at the right.

First Line Indent

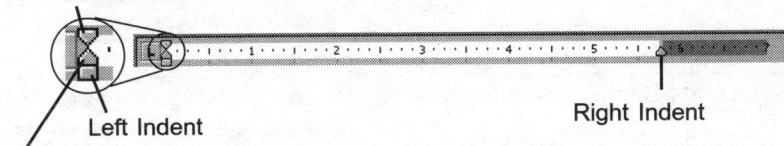

Left Indent

Right Indent

Hanging Indent

- To set the indent you require drag the appropriate indent marker along the ruler to the correct position.

To help improve accuracy when setting indents using the ruler, you can display the exact position of your indent on the ruler as you drag it along.

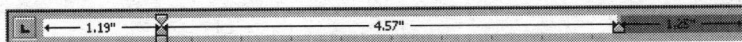

- Hold the **[Alt]** key down while you click and drag.

3.13 Tabs

Tabs are used to align your text horizontally on the typing line. If you want to type up a list of names and telephone numbers you could use tabs to align each column.

The default tabs are set every ½ inch along the ruler – the small dark grey marks along the bottom edge of the ruler indicate their positions.

Each time you press the **[Tab]** key on your keyboard the insertion point jumps forward to the next tab position that is set. The default tabs have left alignment – when you enter your text or numbers the left edge is at the tab position.

Tabs can be aligned to the left, right, centre or decimal character.

Tab	Position of data	Possible usage
Left	The left edge is at tab	Any text or numbers
Right	The right edge is at tab	Text, or numbers you want to line up on the unit
Centre	Centred under the tab	Anything
Decimal	Decimal point under tab	Figures that you want to line up on the decimal point

If you need to use tabs and the pre-set ones are not what you require, you must set tabs at the positions you need them.

Using the ruler

To set a tab

1 Select the type of tab – click the tab style button to the left of the ruler until you get the alignment option required

   L Left   **⊥** Centre   **⌐** Right   **⊥** Decimal

2 Point to the lower half of the ruler and click – your tab is set

To move a tab
- Drag it along the ruler to its correct position.

To delete a tab
- Drag it down off the ruler, and drop it.

USING THE TABS DIALOG BOX

1. Open the **Format** menu and choose **Tabs**
2. Enter the **Tab** stop position
3. Select the **Alignment**
4. Click **Set**
5. Repeat until all your tabs are set
6. Click **OK**

In the Tabs dialog box, there is another option – **Bar**. If you choose this, a vertical line is inserted at the tab position as you enter your data.

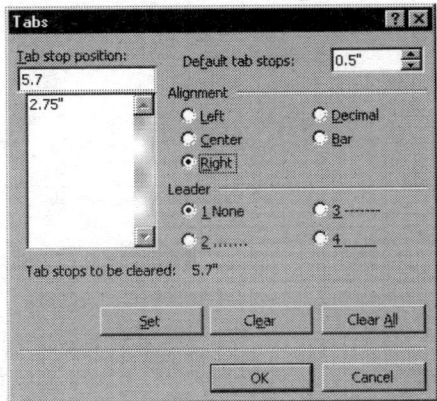

Leader characters

Leader characters are useful to guide the eye along the line when your columns are not close together. They can be set through the Tabs dialog box. Simply choose one before you click **Set.**

In the example on the next page, a centre tab was set at 2.75" for the heading NEWSLETTER, and a right tab was set at 5.7" for the date. The issue number is at the left margin.

Underneath the paragraph that says CONTENTS, the centre tab was removed, and a leader character added to the tab at 5.7" (in the Tabs dialog box).

Left margin   Centre tab   Right tab

Issue 24	NEWSLETTER	November 1997

CONTENTS

3.14 Format Painter

If you need to apply the same formatting to different pieces of text throughout your document, you could use the Format Painter to 'paint' the formatting onto your text.

To use the Format Painter:

1 Select some text that has been formatted using the options you want to 'paint' onto other text

2 Click the Format Painter tool

3 Click and drag over the text you want to 'paint' the formatting on to

If you want to paint the formats onto several separate pieces of text, lock the Format Painter on by double clicking on it. When you are done, click the Format Painter tool again to unlock it.

3.15 Summary

We have discussed many of the formatting options available in Word in this chapter. You have been introduced to:

- Formatting text to make it bold, underlined or in italics.
- Changing the font style, size and colour.
- Highlighting text.
- The Font dialog box.
- Paragraph fromatting techniques.
- Non-printing characters.
- Alignment and line spacing options.
- Applying borders and shading to paragraphs.
- Creating bulleted and numbered lists.
- Customising the bullets in your list.
- Indenting text from the left and right margins.
- Aligning text with tabs.
- Format Painter.

4

SECTIONS AND PAGE LAYOUT

4.1 Aims of this chapter

In this chapter we will discuss sections and some of the page layout options available in Word. By the end of this chapter you will know how to change the page layout of the whole document, or just part of it. We will discuss margins, page orientation (portrait and landscape), columns (newspaper style) and page borders.

4.2 Sections

Sections are used in every Word document. Up until now, the documents we have looked at have consisted of one section only.

If you look at the left side of the Status bar, you will notice that it displays information about the current position of the insertion point within your document.

In this example, the insertion point is currently in Page 1, Section 1 of a 5-page document. Page 1   Sec 1   1/5

Many documents will contain only one section – others may have several.

You may need to divide a document up into different sections for a variety of reasons:

- Part of the document has a different orientation – for example some of the pages are landscape rather than portrait.
- Some of the pages within your document may need different margin settings.
- You might want to set up a page to display a different number of columns on different parts of the page – perhaps for a newsletter layout.

When you opt to change a page layout feature and apply it from this point forward in a dialog box, Word automatically inserts a section break for you. You can also insert section breaks whenever you need to using the **Break** dialog box.

To insert a section break:

1 Choose **Break** from the **Insert** menu

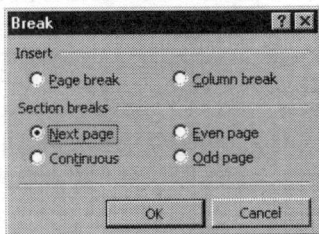

2 Select the **Section break** option

3 Click **OK**

Next Page	Inserts a section break at the insertion point and starts the next section at the top of the next page
Continuous	Inserts a section break at the insertion point, and starts the next section immediately
Even Page	Inserts a section break and starts the next section on the next even numbered page
Odd Page	Inserts a section break and starts the next section on the next odd numbered page

- You can also insert page breaks in the **Break** dialog box – page breaks are discussed fully in Chapter 8, 'Multi-page documents'.

Section breaks are always displayed in Normal view. You can also display them in Page Layout view if you show your non-printing characters.

Once you have inserted a section break, you can format each section individually. You can tell which section your insertion point is in by checking the section indicator on the Status bar.

To change the formatting of a section:

1 Place the insertion point within the section you want to format
2 Make the changes required
• Margins (see 4.3 below)
• Orientation (see 4.4 below)
• Number of columns (see 4.5 below)
• Page borders (see 4.6 below)
3 Click **OK**

To remove a section break:

1 Select the section break (show your non-printing characters if necessary)
2 Press **[Delete]**

When you remove a section break, the section that was above the break adopts the formatting of the one that was below.

4.3 Margins

Margins are the white space between the edge of your paper and the text area. When you create a blank document in Word the margins are automatically set at 1" top and bottom, 1.25" right and left. You can change the margin position for all or part of the document.

USING THE PAGE SETUP DIALOG BOX

The easiest place to change your margins is through the Page Setup dialog box.

1 Open the **File** menu and choose **Page Setup...**
2 Select the **Margins** tab
3 Edit the margin fields as required
4 Specify the area of your document you want to apply the changes to in the **Apply to:** field.
   Select:

- **This section** if you want to change the settings just for the section the insertion point is in (this option only appears if your document consists of more than one section)

- **Whole document** if you want every page on your document to take on the new settings

- **This point forward** if you want to change the setting from the insertion point onwards – a Section break is inserted into your document automatically when you choose **This point forward** in the **Apply to:** field.

5 Click **OK**

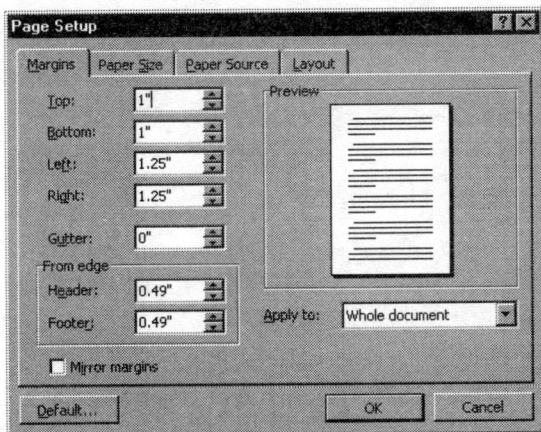

USING THE RULER

You can also change your margins using the ruler. You must be in Page Layout view if you want to change the margins using this method.

In Page Layout view, the dark grey area on the ruler indicates the margin area – the white area shows the typing area.

The top and bottom margin areas are displayed when you are at the top and bottom of the page respectively.

To change the margins using the ruler:

1 Go into Page Layout view (if necessary)

2 Position the mouse pointer where the dark grey and white areas meet – the mouse pointer changes to a double-headed arrow, and a prompt tells you which margin you are over. (It can be a bit tricky getting the Left Margin prompt as the indent markers are in the same area)

3 Click and drag the margin to its new position

If you want to see the exact measurements for the margins you are setting and the measurement between the margins, hold the **[Alt]** key down as you drag the margin.

When you change your margins using the ruler, they will affect the section your insertion point is in. If your document consists of one section, the whole document will be affected. If your document consists of more than one section, only the section that the insertion point is currently in will be affected.

GUTTERS AND MIRRORS!

If you are going to bind your document, you can set a **Gutter Margin** to allow for the binding, on the Margins tab of the Page Setup dialog box.

If your binding method is going to take up half an inch down the left edge of your pages, set the gutter to 0.5". This amount of space will be left at the edge of the page before the left margin is calculated – the distance between the margins is reduced automatically to allow for the gutter.

If you are going to print your document double sided, then bind it, set your gutter and select the **Mirror Margins** checkbox. The left and right margin fields change to outside and inside margins – the gutter is down the inside margin.

4.4 Orientation

The orientation of a page can be *Portrait* or *Landscape*. The default orientation is Portrait. You can change the orientation of your pages for all of your document or for part of it as required.

To change orientation:

1 Open the **File** menu and choose **Page Setup...**
2 Select the **Paper Size** tab
3 Choose the **Orientation** required
4 Specify the area of your document you want to apply the changes to in the **Apply to:** field.

Select:

- **Whole document** if you want every page on your document to take on the new settings.

- **This point forward** if you want to change the setting from the insertion point onwards - a section break is inserted into your document automatically when you choose **This point forward** in the **Apply to:** field.

- **This section** if you only want to change the settings for the section the insertion point is in (this option only appears if your document consists of more than one section).

5 Click **OK**

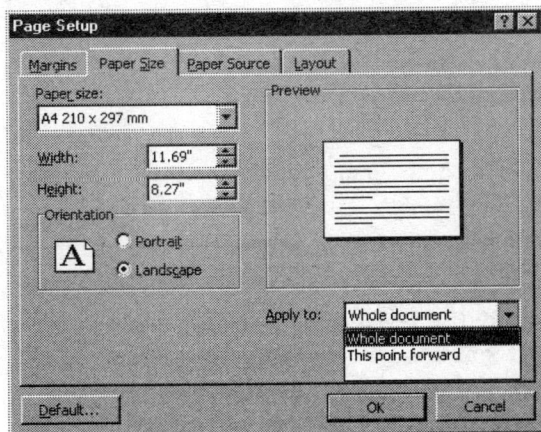

If you choose **This point forward** in the **Apply to:** field, Word will insert a section break at the insertion point, and move on to the next page.

You may find you end up with a document that has several sections, changing from one orientation to another as your document develops.

4.5 Columns

Most documents have the text displayed in one column, running across the page from margin to margin.

If you create leaflets, newsletters or advertising 'fliers', you may want your text to appear in several columns across your page.

If you intend to have a different number of columns on different parts of the same page, you must divide the page up using **Continuous** section breaks.

To insert a continuous section break:

1 Place the insertion point where you want the section break

2 Choose **Break** from the **Insert** menu

3 Select **Continuous**

4 Click **OK**

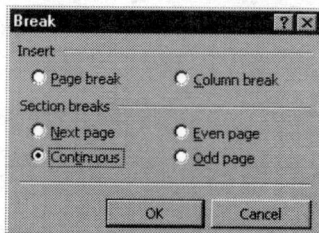

You must then format each section to display the number of columns required.

1 Place the insertion point within the section you want to edit
2 Open the **Format** menu and choose **Columns**
3 Specify the number or columns required – you can have up to 11 if you use the **Number of columns** field
4 Select any other options required, e.g. **Line between columns**

- If you don't want your columns all the same width, deselect the Equal column width checkbox and set the Width (width of the column) and Spacing (distance between columns) options as required.

5   Click **OK**

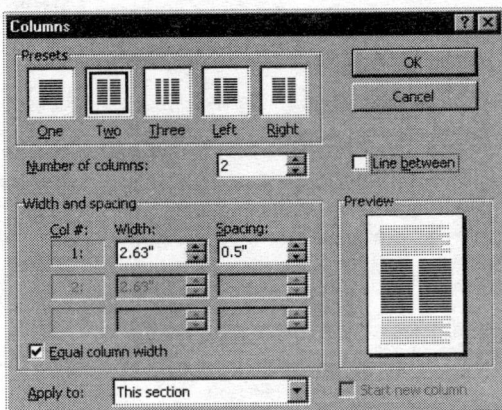

When you type your text into a page that has multiple columns set up, the text flows down to the bottom of the first column on the page, then wraps to the top of the next column. It then fills the second column, then wraps to the next one and so on.

You can force a column break if you don't want the text to run to the bottom of the page.

To insert a manual column break:

1   Place the insertion point where you want to insert a column break

2   Open the **Insert** menu and choose **Break...**

3   Select **Column**

4   Click **OK**

The picture below has a continuous section break inserted after the heading. Section 1 is formatted to display one column – this allows the heading to run across the whole page.

Section 2 is formatted to display 2 columns. The text has wrapped automatically at the bottom of the first column and flowed to the top of column 2.

Section 1 – one full width column

Section break here

Section 2 – two columns

Letter from the editor

This layout illustrates the use of a continuous section break - the heading is in Section 1, which is in a single column.

The text and picture are in Section 2, which has a 2-column layout.

The text and picture are in Section 2, which has a 2-column layout.

You can have a maximum of 11 columns across your page.

You can find out how to insert a picture in Chapter 10.

This layout illustrates the use of a continuous section break - the heading is in Section 1, which is in a single column.

The Editor

You can find out how to insert a picture in Chapter 11.

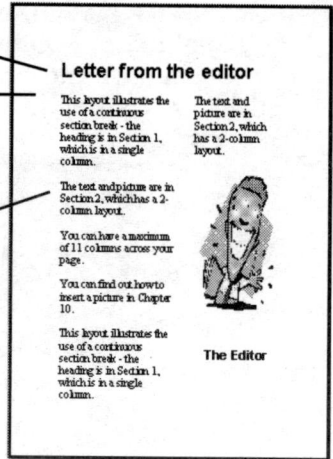

4.6 Page borders

If you want to add a special effect to a page, have a look through the Page Border options. Page borders can be very effective on menus, newsletters, programmes, invitations, etc.

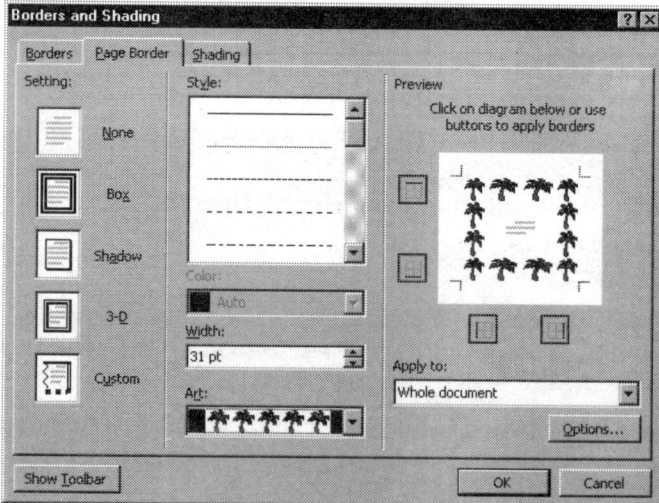

To apply a page border:

1 Choose **Borders and Shading** from the **Format** menu

2 Select the **Page Border** tab

3 Select the border style required – either use the basic line styles, or try out the Art options

4 Click **OK**

4.7 Summary

In this chapter we have discussed:

- Sections.
- Margins.
- Orientation.
- Columns.
- Page Borders.

5

AUTOMATING TASKS

5.1 Aims of this chapter

In this chapter we will consider some ways in which you can automate the way you work in Word. We will discuss AutoText, AutoCorrect, AutoComplete and some of the Wizards that are available to you.

5.2 AutoText

How often do you type the same text or insert the same picture (see Chapter 11) into a document? It could be your name and address, an address you use often, a department name, a circulation list, clauses in contracts or your company logo.

If you retype the same text regularly, you should consider making the text into an AutoText entry. You can then insert the text into your document with a few keystrokes or mouse clicks – even if the AutoText entry is several paragraphs long.

To create an AutoText entry:

1 Select the text or picture you want to make into an AutoText entry – include the paragraph mark at the end of the paragraph if you want the paragraph formatting saved with the AutoText entry

2 Open the **Insert** menu, choose **AutoText**, then **New** (or press **[Alt]-[F3]**)

3 Either accept the name suggested or edit it as required

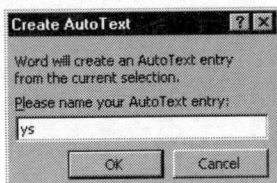

4 Click **OK**

> **Create AutoText** ? ✕
>
> Word will create an AutoText entry from the current selection.
>
> Please name your AutoText entry:
>
> ys
>
> OK   Cancel

To insert an AutoText entry:

If you know the name of the AutoText entry you want to insert

1 Position the insertion point where you want the AutoText entry to appear

2 Type in the AutoText entry name (don't put a space at the end of it)

3 Press **[F3]**

If you don't know the name of the AutoText entry

1 Position the insertion point where you want the AutoText

2 Open the **Insert** menu and select **AutoText**

AUTOCOMPLETE

You may have noticed that Word suggests your AutoText entry as you enter the AutoText name into your document.

This is the *AutoComplete* tip. If you want to insert the entry, press **[Enter]** or **[F3]** when the tip appears. If you don't want to insert the AutoText entry, ignore the tip and keep typing.

You can switch this feature on and off on the **AutoText** tab in the **AutoCorrect** dialog box. Select or de-select the **Show AutoComplete tip for AutoText and dates** checkbox at the top of the dialog box as required.

---

3 Choose **AutoText**

4 On the **AutoText** tab in the **AutoCorrect** dialog box, select the entry required from the list

5 Click **Insert**

Turn off the AutoComplete tip if you prefer to work without it

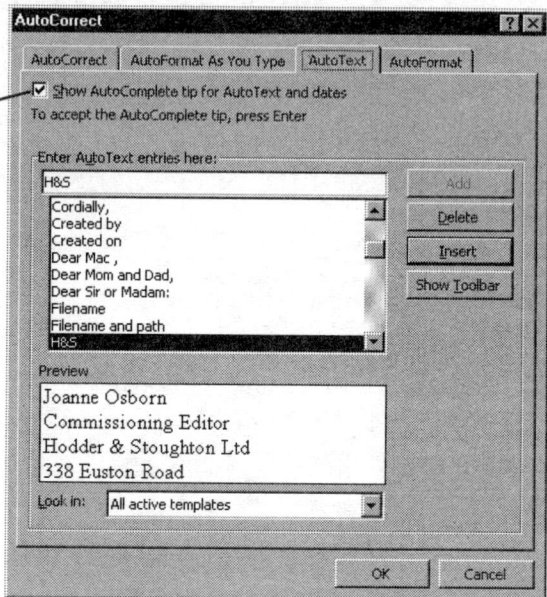

or

1 Position the insertion point where you want the AutoText entry to appear

2 Open the **Insert** menu and select **AutoText**

3 Choose an entry category

4 Click on the entry

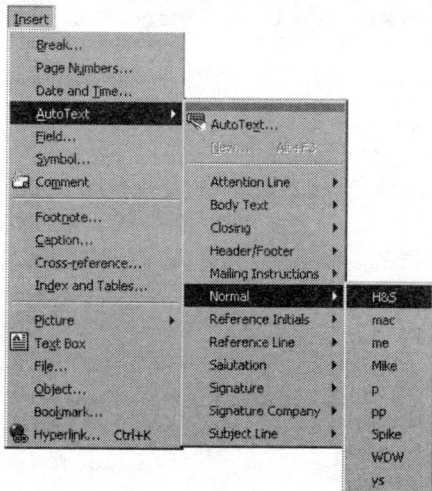

To delete an AutoText entry:

1 Open the **Insert** menu and select **AutoText**
2 Choose **AutoText**
3 On the **AutoText** tab in the **AutoCorrect** dialog box, select the entry to be deleted from the list
4 Click **Delete**

To redefine (edit) an AutoText entry:

1 Insert the AutoText entry you want to edit into your document
2 Make the changes required – e.g. add, delete, format
3 Select the edited AutoText entry in your document
4 Press **[Alt]-[F3]**
5 Enter the original AutoText entry name
6 Click **OK**
7 At the prompt, click **Yes** to replace the old version with the new

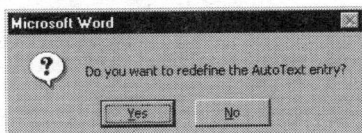

To rename an AutoText entry:

1 Open the **Tools** menu and choose **Templates and Add-ins**
2 Click **Organizer**
3 Select the **AutoText** tab

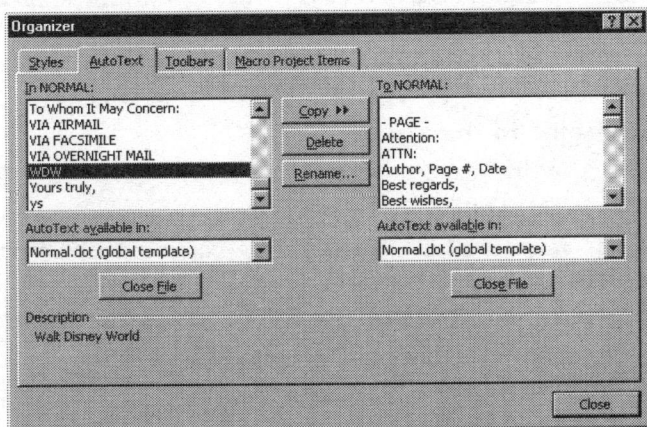

4 Choose the entry you want to rename from the **In** list

5 Click **Rename**

6 Enter the new name for the entry in the **Rename** dialog box

7 Click **OK**

8 Click **Close**

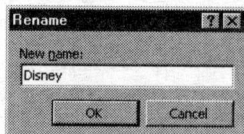

5.3 Spike

The Spike is a special AutoText entry that you can use to rearrange the text and graphics within your document.

The Spike is a container into which you can collect text and graphics from non-adjacent locations in your document. Once you have collected the text and graphics, you can insert the contents of the Spike wherever you wish. You may find that there are times that you can use the Spike to save you several separate cut and paste operations.

The text and graphics are added to the Spike in the order you want them to reappear in your document. When you add an item to the Spike, it is deleted from your document. You then empty the contents of the Spike at the desired location.

To add items to the Spike:

1 Select the first item required

2 Press **[Ctrl]-[F3]**

3 Repeat steps 1 and 2 until you've collected up everything required

To empty the contents of the Spike into your document:

1 Position the insertion point where you want the contents of the Spike to appear

2 Press **[Ctrl]-[Shift]-[F3]**

You must empty the spike before you start building up a new group of items – if you don't empty it, anything you add is appended to what's already there.

However, you can insert the contents of the Spike into your document without emptying the Spike if you wish.

To insert the contents of the Spike without emptying it:

1 Position the insertion point where you want the contents of the Spike to appear
2 Open the **Insert** menu and choose **AutoText**
3 Click **AutoText**
4 Select **Spike** from the list – a preview will appear in the Preview window
5 Click **Insert**

5.4 AutoText field

If you are adding the same text many times to a long document – a clause to a contract or disclaimer to a legal document – and the contents of the clause or disclaimer have not yet been finalised, you can still use an AutoText entry.

However, when the wording in the clause or disclaimer becomes final, it would be more efficient to have the AutoText entry updated automatically throughout your document, rather than you have to go to each occurrence and delete the old version and insert the new one.

It is possible to do this if you enter your AutoText entry as a *field* rather than a normal AutoText entry. A field is a placeholder or code that is used to indicate where the data should appear, but the actual contents of the placeholder can be updated automatically.

You will meet many different types of field in Word. An AutoText field can be updated automatically if the contents of the AutoText entry change – which might save you a lot of work in some cases.

To insert an AutoText entry as a field:

1 Place the insertion point where you want the AutoText field to appear

2 Open the **Insert** menu and choose **Field...**

3 Select *Links and References* in the **Categories** list

4 Choose *AutoText* in the **Field names** list

5 Click **Options...**

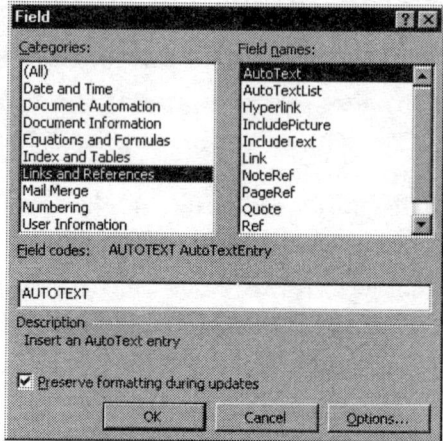

6 Select the AutoText entry you wish to enter as a **Field**

7 Click **Add to Field**

8 Click **OK** to close the Field Options dialog box

9 Click **OK** to close the Field dialog box

The contents of the AutoText entry are added to your document as a field.

If the contents of the AutoText entry are edited, you will need to update the AutoText fields so that they show the modified version of the AutoText entry. You can update your AutoText fields individually, collectively or when you print.

When you redefine the contents of the AutoText entry, as described in 5.2 above, the AutoText fields will not pick up the edited version of the AutoText entry automatically.

To update an individual AutoText field:

1 Click anywhere within the AutoText field you wish to update

2 Press **[F9]**

To update all your AutoText fields at the same time:

1 Select the whole document – **[Ctrl]-[A]**

2 Press **[F9]**

3 Deselect the text

To update your AutoText fields when you print:

1 Open the **Tools** menu and choose **Options**

2 Select the **Print** tab

3 Select the **Update Fields** checkbox

4 Click **OK**

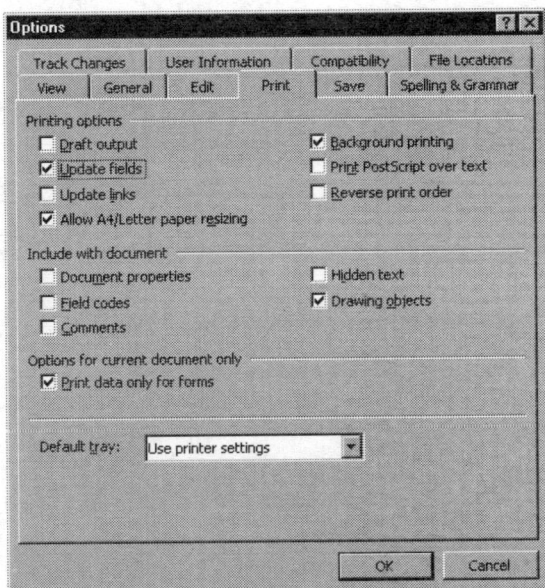

Your fields will be updated the next time you print your document.

5.5 AutoCorrect

The AutoCorrect feature helps you correct your 'typos' (typing errors) quickly. Some typing errors are very common – Word recognises many of them and corrects them automatically.

If you type in 'hte' you will find that Word automatically changes it to 'the', or when you type 'adn' it becomes 'and'. If you start typing a new sentence without using an initial capital on the first word, Word will fix it!

If you tend to make specific typing errors that Word doesn't recognise, you can easily add these to Word's recognised list.

To display the list of AutoCorrect entries already set up:

1 Open the **Tools** menu

2 Choose **AutoCorrect**

The dialog box shows the list of entries, and the AutoCorrect options that are selected.

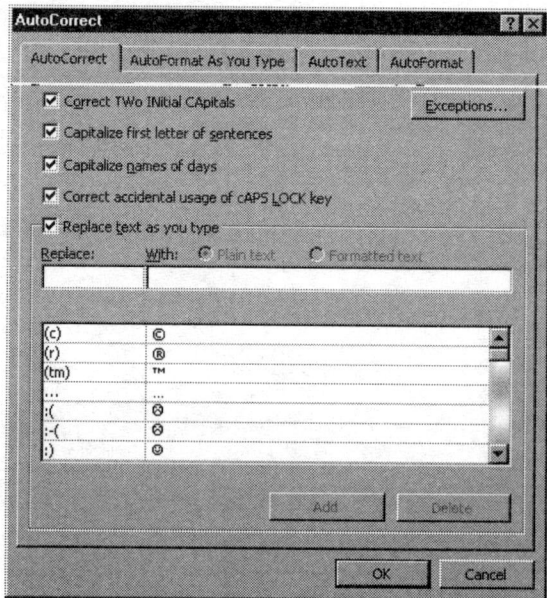

To add an entry to the list:

1   Open the **Tools** menu and choose **AutoCorrect**
2   Enter the text you want to be automatically replaced in the **Replace** field
3   Key in the text you want to replace it with in the **With** field
4   Click **Add**
5   Click **OK**

To delete an entry from the list:

1   Open the **Tools** menu and choose **AutoCorrect**
2   Select the entry you wish to delete
3   Click **Delete**

To redefine (replace) an entry in the list:

1   Open the **Tools** menu and choose **AutoCorrect**
2   Select the entry you want to redefine
3   Edit it as required in the **Replace** and **With** fields
4   Click **Replace**
5   At the **Redefine** prompt, click **Yes**

SPELL CHECK AND AUTOCORRECT

You will notice an **AutoCorrect** button appears in the **Spelling and Grammar** dialog box when you spell check your document.

To add your error and correction to the AutoCorrect list:

1   Select the correct word from the suggestion list
2   Click **AutoCorrect**

───── 5.5 Document Wizards ─────

Up until now, any documents we have created have been based on the Blank Document template, which gives a blank A4 sized sheet on which to enter your text.

We will consider other template options later, but, for the time being, if you want to create a letter, memo, fax or résumé document, you might like to try a Wizard to step you through the process of setting up the document.

We'll try a couple of the document wizards. This is for a memo:

1 Open the **File** menu and choose **New...**
2 At the **New** dialog box, select the **Memos** tab and click on the **Memo Wizard**
3 Click **OK**

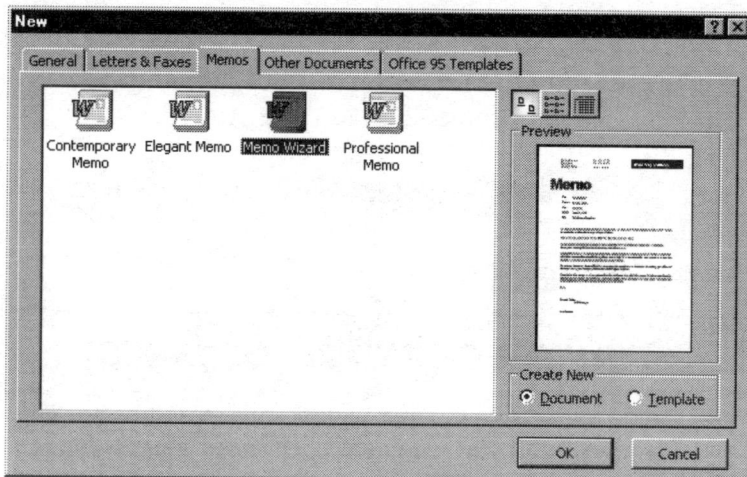

4 Work through the Wizard, clicking **Next** after each step
5 When you reach the final step, click **Finish**
- At the **cc** field, 'Click here' and type in details if necessary – otherwise 'Click here' and press the **[Delete]** key on your keyboard to get rid of the prompt.
- If you included a priority field – click and type in your priority message.
- To type in the body of your memo – 'Click here' as prompted, and type.

The headers and footers at the top and bottom of each page are inserted automatically with the detail you selected at the Header/Footer step in the Wizard.

This time try out the **Letter Wizard.**

1 Open the **File** menu and choose New...

2 Select the **Letters & Faxes** tab

3 Choose **Letter Wizard** and click **OK**

4 At the Office Assistant prompt, select **Send one letter**

5 Complete each step of the wizard as required

6 Click **Finish** when you reach the end

7 The Office Assistant will return to ask if an envelope or label is require – select the option you want (or rerun the Letter Wizard if you need to change anything)

- In this example, I chose **Make an envelope**. The Letter Wizard takes the recipient's address and copies it onto an envelope page at the beginning of your letter.

8 Select the text under the salutation, delete it and type in the body of your letter

Do more with the letter?

● Make an envelope

● Make a mailing label

● Rerun Letter Wizard

● Cancel

24 June 1997

John MacPherson
24 High Street
INVERNESS
Highland Region

Dear John,
SUBJECT: YOUR VISIT TO EDINBURGH

Type your letter here. To add, remove, or change letter elements, choose Letter Wizard from the Tools menu.

Sincerely,

Moira Stephen

ST STEPHEN HOUSE
EDINBURGH
EH5 4AR

John MacPherson
24 High Street
INVERNESS
Highland Region

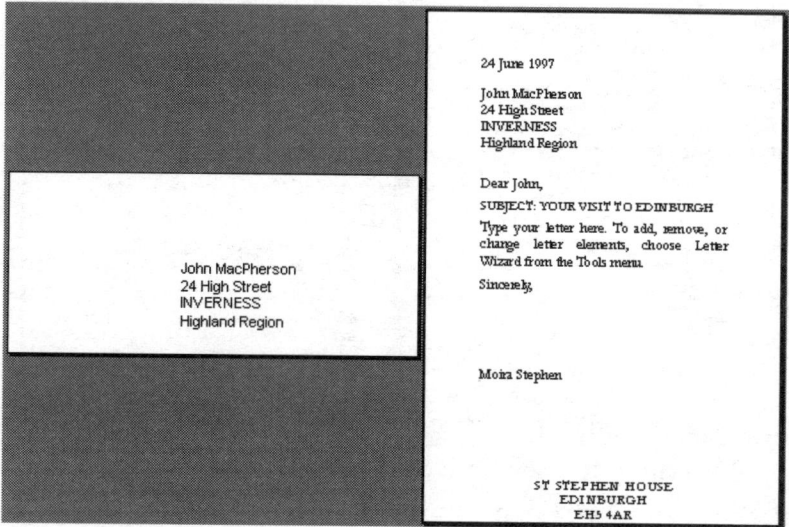

If you need to edit any of the elements automatically inserted by the Letter Wizard:

1 Open the **Tools** menu
2 Choose **Letter Wizard...**
3 Select the tab that contains the element(s) you wish to edit
4 Make the changes required
5 Click **OK**

If you think the document wizards would be useful, try out the Fax Wizard and the Résumé Wizard. Experiment with the options available until you find a style that appeals to you.

5.7 Summary

In this chapter we have discussed some options that can help improve your efficiency by automating some tasks. We have discussed how you can:

- Create, use and manage AutoText entries.
- Use the Spike to collect text up before inserting it at a new location.
- Automate the updating of AutoText entries by using AutoText fields.
- Add, replace and delete AutoCorrect entries.
- Create a memo using a document Wizard.
- Create a letter using a document Wizard.

6

STYLES

—————— 6.1 Aims of this chapter ——————

In this chapter we will discuss styles. You'll find out why styles are important (and very useful). You can use Word's own styles or modify the styles set up in Word to suit your own requirements. You can also create your own styles – it's up to you.

—————— 6.2 Putting on the style ——————

What is a style?

A style is simply a collection of formatting options that you *name*. There are 2 kinds of style:

- **Character styles** – where the formatting options are taken from those in the Font dialog box.
- **Paragraph styles** – where the formatting options can be a combination of font and paragraph formatting commands.

Why should you use styles?

SPEED

Once you've collected your formatting options into a style, you can then apply the style to your text, rather than apply each formatting option individually. If you have more than a couple of formatting options stored in your style, it is usually quicker to apply a style than apply each formatting option individually.

CONSISTENCY

If you collect the formatting options you want to use into a style, then apply the style to your text and paragraphs as required, the formatting throughout your document will be more consistent.

You've been using styles since you started using Word – but you probably didn't notice. The formatting that your font and paragraph have are determined by a style called *Normal*.

The default Normal style is a paragraph style that is left aligned and in single line spacing. The characters are formatted using the Times New Roman font, size 10.

At the left of the Formatting toolbar, the **Style** box Normal tells you the name of the style that is currently being applied to your text.

—— 6.3 Styles in a blank document ——

Each document you create in Word will have several styles already set up.

To display the styles available in your current document:

- Click the drop-down arrow to the right of the Style box to display the styles list.

The styles listed are available to you each time you create a new blank document.

The first four styles in the list are Paragraph styles, the last one is a Character style (the icon to the right of the style name indicates whether it is a Paragraph ¶ or Character **a** style).

Normal	▼
Heading 1	📰 ¶ 14 pt
Heading 2	📰 ¶ 12 pt
Heading 3	📰 ¶ 12 pt
Normal	📰 ¶ 12 pt
Default Paragraph Font	📰 a 10 pt

These styles are stored in the Blank Document template and are automatically available to you in every new document you create based on this template.

You can either apply a style to text as you key the text in, or enter the text and then go back to select it and apply the style.

To apply a style to new text:

1 Click the drop-down arrow to the right of the Style box to display the style list
2 Select the style you want to use – click on it
3 Type in your text
4 Press **[Enter]**

Heading 1 - Arial, size 14, bold, left aligned, spacing before 12 pt, spacing after 3 pt

Heading 2 - Arial, size 12, bold, italic, left aligned, spacing before 12 pt, spacing after 3 pt

Heading 3 - Arial, size 12, left aligned, spacing before 12 pt, spacing after 3 pt

When you press **[Enter]** after each of the Heading styles above, the paragraph style used for the following paragraph returns to Normal automatically.

To apply a style to existing text:

1 Select the text you want to apply a style to
2 Click the drop-down arrow to the right of the Style box to display the style list
3 Select the style you want to use

LOTS AND LOTS OF STYLES

Many styles are already set up in Word – far more than those displayed in the style list. Different styles are recorded in the various templates (patterns on which your documents are based), and are automatically available to you when you create a document using these templates.

You can however, display a list of *all* the styles from all the different templates if you wish. To do so, hold down the **[Shift]** key and click the drop-down arrow to display the style list. All the styles should be there. You can select any one of them – once you've selected a style it will be added to the style list in your document.

───── 6.4 Editing an existing style ─────

Editing from within a document

If you think that you might like to use styles (and I'd recommend that you do), but the formatting is not quite what you want, you can easily edit any of the styles that are already set up.

Let's say you wanted the *Heading 1* style to be size 16, centred with a top and bottom border and 15% shading.

1 Apply the Heading 1 style to some text
2 Edit the formatting as required
3 Select the text again (include the paragraph mark if you want the paragraph formatting included in your style – in this example that would be the alignment, borders and shading)
4 Click inside the **Style** box
5 Press **[Enter]**
6 Select *Update the style to reflect recent changes?* at the **Modify Style** prompt

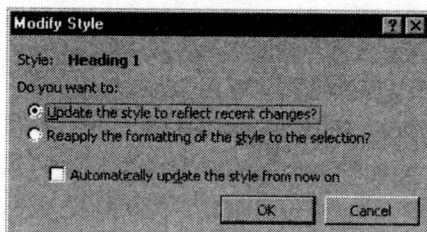

7 Click **OK**

When you edit a style, any text within your document that has the style already applied to it will be updated to reflect the new formatting recorded in the style.

MODIFY STYLE PROMPT

If you don't want the prompt to appear when you edit styles this way, select the **Automatically update the style from now on** checkbox the next time the **Modify Style** prompt appears.

You can switch the prompt back on again if you want to. Choose **Style** from the **Format** menu, click **Modify...** and clear the **Automatically update** checkbox in the **Modify Style** dialog box.

Editing from the Style dialog box

The method above is perhaps the quickest way to redefine a style. However, you may prefer to use the Style dialog box.

To edit a style using the Style dialog box:

1 Open the **Format** menu and choose **Style**
2 The styles listed in the Style dialog box are those currently in use in your document – if necessary, select an alternative option from the **List** field to display the style you want to edit
3 Select the style you want to change
4 Click **Modify...**
5 Click the **Format...** button and choose the formatting option
6 Format the style as required

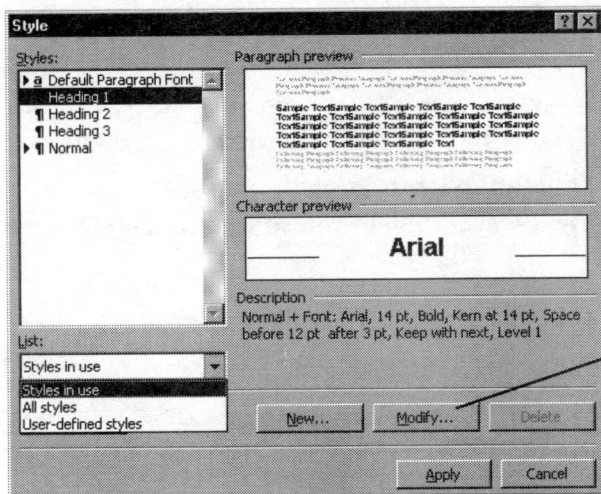

Click **Modify**
to reformat
the style

Check **Add to template**
to make the new style
available in future
documents

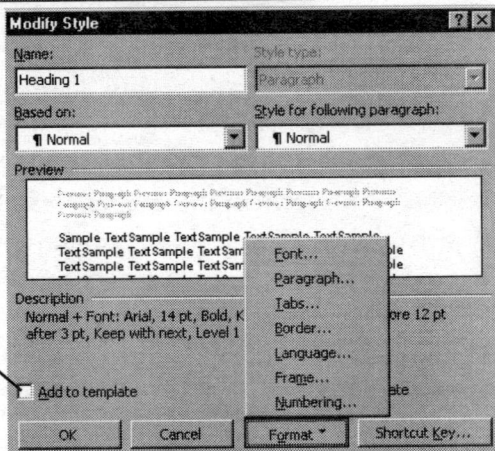

7 Click **OK** to return to the **Modify Style** dialog box

8 Repeat steps 5 – 7 until you've made all the changes required

9 Select the **Add to Template** checkbox if you want your edited style available in each new document you create using the current template

10 Click **OK** to return to the **Style** dialog box

11 Click **Apply** or **Close**

6.5 Creating a new style

Styles that you create are called User-defined styles. The easiest way to create a User-defined style is from within your document.

To create a style from within your document:

1 Apply the formats you want to record into a style to some existing text

2 Select the text

3 Click in the **Style** box

4 Type in the name you want your style to have

5 Press **[Enter]**

A style created in this way is stored with your document, not the template on which your document was based.

If you want to add the style to the template so that it is available automatically to all other documents based on the current template, or give it a keyboard shortcut, you must go into the **Modify Style** dialog box.

To add your style to the document template:

1 Choose **Style** from the **Format** menu

2 Select the style you want to add from the **Styles** list

3 Click **Modify...**

4 Select the **Add to Template** checkbox

5 Set a Shortcut Key if you wish – click **Shortcut Key...** and enter your shortcut in the **Press new shortcut key:** field in the **Customize Keyboard** dialog box.

   Click **Assign** and then **Close**.

• You will be warned if the shortcut you choose is already assigned to another function – think carefully before re-assigning a shortcut – are you sure you don't already use the shortcut for something else?

6 Click **OK**

The next time you create a document using the current template, your style will be displayed in the Style list.

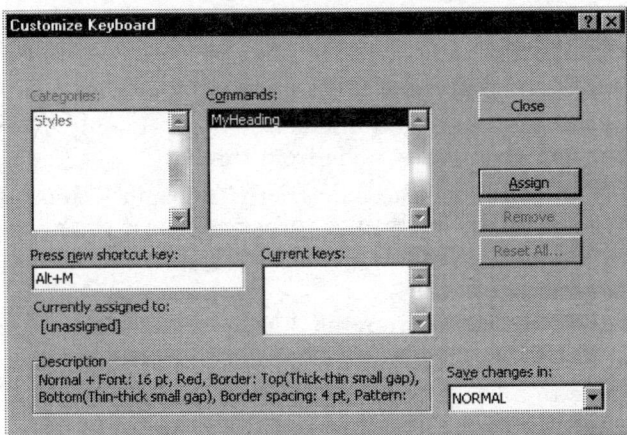

You can also create a new style from the New Style dialog box. If you create your style in the dialog box you can assign it a keyboard shortcut, add it to the template and specify the style of the following paragraph all at the same time.

To create a style from the New Style dialog box:

1 If you haven't a document open, open one or create a new document

2 Open the **Format** menu and choose **Style**

3 Click **New...**

If there is an existing style that is close to what you want, use that as the base

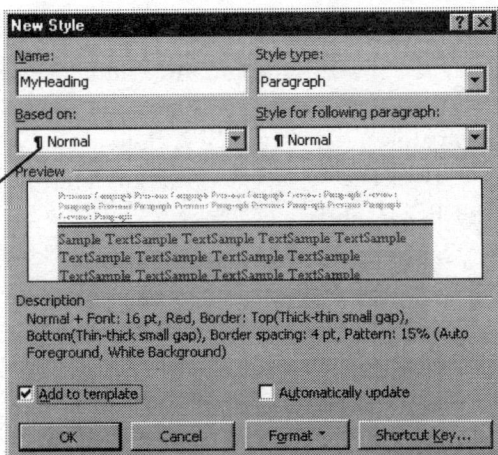

4 Give your style a name – something more appropriate than *Style1*

5 Set the **Style type** required – *paragraph* or *character*

6 Select the style your new one is based on – usually *Normal* – but you can choose any style from the list

7 Specify the style for the following paragraph – this defaults to the same as the one you are creating, but if you are setting up a style for headings, you may want it to be the next level of heading, or *Normal*

8 Click the **Format** button and specify the formats required

9 Select the **Add to Template** checkbox if you want the style available to all new documents using the current template

10 Give the style a keyboard shortcut if required

11. Click **OK**

12. Click **Close**

6.6 Style management

You can manage User-defined styles by deleting, renaming and copying them as necessary.

To delete a style:

1 Open the **Format** menu and choose **Style**

2 Display the styles you have set up by choosing **User-defined styles** in the style **List** field

3 Select the style you want to delete

4 Click **Delete**

5 Confirm the deletion

6 Close the **Style** dialog box

or

1 Open the **Format** menu and choose **Style**

2 Click **Organizer...**

3 Select the style you want to delete from the lists

4 Click **Delete**

5 Confirm the deletion

6 Close the **Organizer** dialog box

To rename a style:

1 Open the **Format** menu and choose **Style**

2 Click **Organizer...**

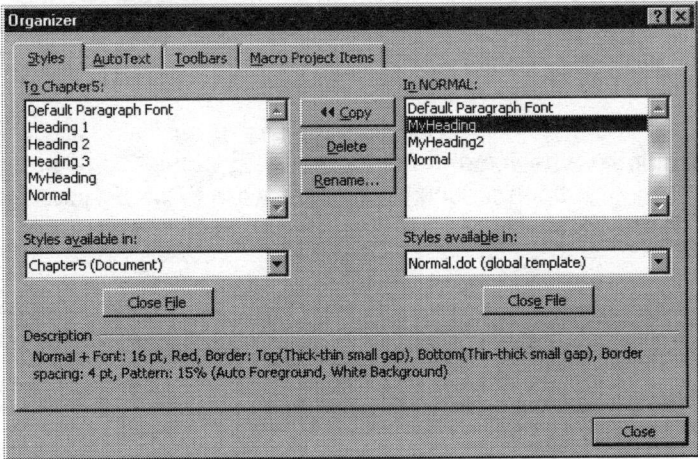

3 If necessary close the file displayed and open the file you require

4 Select the style you wish to rename

5 Click **Rename...**

6 Enter the new name for your style

7 Click **OK**

8 Click **Close** to close the Organizer dialog box

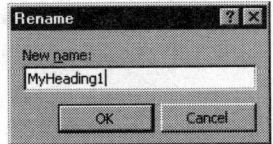

THE ORGANIZER STYLES TAB

It you have a document open when you go into the Organizer dialog box, the styles in the current document and those in the template on which it is based will be listed on the Styles tab.

If you don't want to work with the files that are currently open, you can close either or both in the Organizer dialog box, and open the files required. When you close a file in the Organizer dialog box, the **Close File** button becomes the **Open File** button, and you can click this and go on to locate and open the file you want to use.

When you go to open a file from the Organizer dialog box, the default file type listed in the Open dialog box is *Template*. If you want to open a document, change the **Files of Type** field to *Word documents*.

You can copy styles from one file to another using the Organizer dialog box. If you have created some new styles in your document, then decide you should have stored them in the document template, you can quickly copy them over using this method.

To copy a style:

1 Open the **Format** menu and choose **Style**
2 Click **Organizer...**
3 Select the style you want to copy
4 Click **Copy**
5 Close the **Organizer** dialog box

—————— 6.7 Style Gallery ——————

You can preview the styles from any template through the Style Gallery. If you wish, you can apply the styles from the template you preview, to the current document.

1 Open the **Format** menu and choose **Style Gallery...**

2 Select the template you want to preview the styles from

3 Do you want to preview the styles from the template using your current Document, an Example or Style samples? Select from the Preview options listed

• The Preview window displays the styles using the chosen option.

4 If you want to apply the styles from the template to your current document, click **OK**, if not click **Cancel**

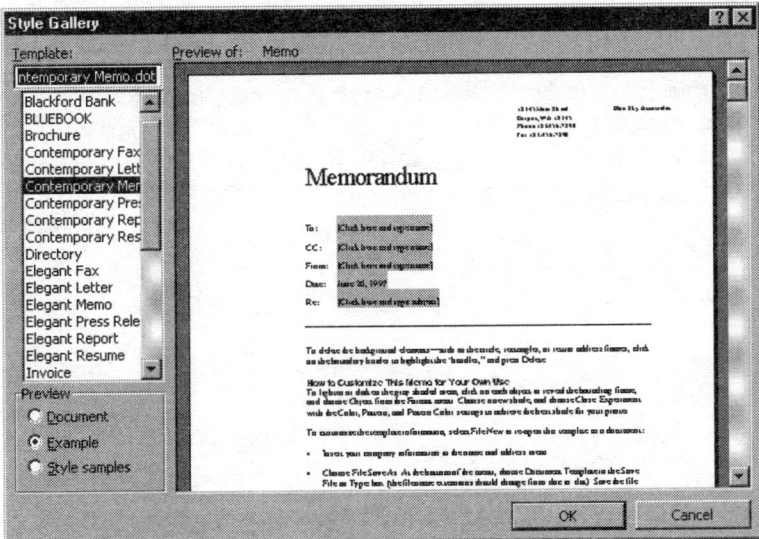

HAS IT CHANGED?

If you have not used styles in your current document, and you opt to preview the styles using the Document option, there will be little or no change in the preview window.

However, if you have formatted your document using styles, and the template you select in the Style Gallery has styles of the same name but with different formatting, the changes to your document may be quite dramatic.

6.8 Summary

In this chapter we have discussed styles. Styles are important for a number of reasons – not least that they improve efficiency by increasing your speed, and ensuring consistency within and across your documents.

You have learnt how to:

- Use the in-built styles that come with Word.
- Edit styles.
- Create your own User-defined styles.
- Manage your User-defined styles by copying, deleting and renaming.
- View styles from different templates through the Style Gallery and apply them to your document.

7

TABLES

7.1 Aims of this chapter

In this chapter you will find out just how useful and versatile tables can be for all kinds of things. Tables can be used when you need to enter text in a parallel column layout, and they can be very useful if you need to design forms. If your table contains numeric data, you can perform basic calculations on that data.

7.2 Table basics

Tables consist of rows and columns. Where a row and column intersect, we have a cell.

To create a table:

1 Place the insertion point where you want your table to appear

2 Click the **Insert Table** tool 🔳 on the Standard toolbar

3 Click and drag over the grid that appears until you get the number of rows and columns required

4 Let go the mouse button – you have an empty table on your page

If you have your non-printing characters displayed, you will notice markers at the end of each cell and row that look a bit like a sun! Don't worry about them – hide your non-printing characters 🔳 if they distract you.

You can move around your table using the keyboard or the mouse.

• Press the **[Tab]** key to move forward to the next cell.

• Hold the **[Shift]** key down and press tab to move back to the previous cell.

or

• Click in the cell you want to move to.

Selecting cells in a table:

• Click and drag over the cells you want to select.

or

1 Click in the corner cell of the range of cells you want to select

2 Point to the cell in the diagonally opposite corner using your mouse

3 Hold the **[Shift]** key down and click

To select a column:

• Click the top gridline or border of the column you want to select (you should get a black arrow pointing downwards).

(To select several adjacent columns, click and drag along the top border).

To select a row:

• Click to the left of the row you want to select.

(To select several adjacent rows, click and drag up or down the row selector area.)

Click to select column ↓

Click to → select row

To select a cell:
- Click just inside the left edge of the cell

Other things to note:
- When you create your table, each column is the same width, and the table stretches across the page.
- When entering text into a cell, you will find that your text automatically wraps once the text reaches the right edge of the cell, and the row deepens to accommodate the text you are entering.
- Text and numbers automatically align to the left of a cell.
- If you press **[Tab]** when the insertion point is in the last cell in the last row of your table, a new row is created.
- You can format your cells, or text within the cells, using the normal formatting commands.

——7.3 Column width and row height——

Column width

In most cases, you won't want all your columns to be the same width – it depends what you're entering into them. You can easily change the column width as required. There are several methods you might like to try out – then use whatever you find easiest.

AUTOFIT

You must have some text or data in your columns to give AutoFit something to work on.

- Double click the border or gridline to the right of the column whose width you want to change.

or

1. Place the insertion anywhere inside the column you want to adjust
2. On the ruler, double click on a **Move Table Column** marker to the right of the column whose width you want to change

Move Table Column markers

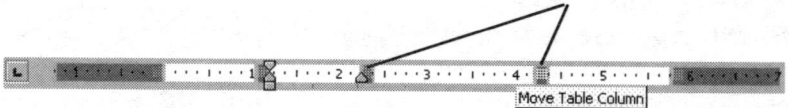

Move Table Column

or

Open the **Table** menu and choose **Cell Height and Width...**
3. Click **AutoFit** on the **Column** tab of the **Cell Height and Width** dialog box

The column width will adjust automatically to give a 'best fit' for that column.

If you need to change columns when you're in the Cell Height and Width dialog box, use the **Previous Column** or **Next Column** buttons to select the column required.

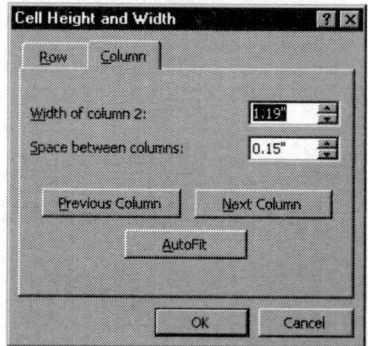

Cell Height and Width

Row | Column

Width of column 2: 1.19"
Space between columns: 0.15"

Previous Column | Next Column

AutoFit

OK | Cancel

MANUAL ADJUSTMENT

1   Position the mouse pointer over the gridline or border to the right of the column you want to adjust

2   Click and drag right the border or gridline as required

or

1   Click and drag the **Move Table Column** marker (on the ruler) which is above the right border of the column you want to adjust

ADDRESS	NOTES	COST
Old Mill Inn 24 Mill Lane Melrose	Delightful retreat in the Scottish borders. Food from 10 am until 10 pm. Excellent lunches and evening meal. Accommodation available. Working waterwheel, herb garden and riverside walks.	Lunches from £4 Dinner from £11.50 Dinner, Bed and Breakfast:£35
Kathy's Kitchen 12 High Street Duns	Excellent family run coffee shop. Soup, baked potatoes, sandwiches etc all day. Delicious home baking!	Various.

You can set the width in the **Cell Height and Width** dialog box:

1   Open the **Cell Height and Width...** dialog box

2   On the **Column** tab, locate the column you want to change the width of

3   Edit the **Width of column** and **Space between columns** fields as required

4   Click **OK**

Row height

Row height can also be adjusted. The row height default is **Auto**, which allows the row to automatically deepen as you enter your text.

However if you are using tables to design forms, you may need to set your row height to a minimum or exact size.

You do this using very similar techniques to those used when adjusting the column width.

1 Open the **Cell Height and Width** dialog box
2 Select the **Row** tab
3 If necessary, use the **Previous Row** or **Next Row** buttons to locate the row you want to adjust
4 Select the height option required in the **Height of rows** field

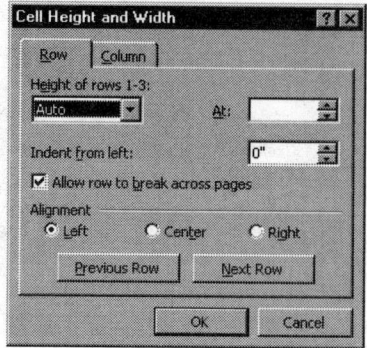

Cell Height and Width

Row | Column

Height of rows 1-3:
Auto   At:

Indent from left: 0"

☑ Allow row to break across pages

Alignment
● Left   ○ Center   ○ Right

Previous Row   Next Row

OK   Cancel

Auto   Automatically deepens the row to accommodate the cell with the most lines.

At Least Sets a minimum row size (you set the size in the **At** field) If you enter text that exceeds the size set, Word will adjust the height to accommodate it.

Exactly Sets an exact size (you set the size in the **At** field) If you enter text that exceeds the size set, Word will display only what will fit in the row height specified.

5 Click **OK**

If you are in Page Layout view, Adjust Table Row markers are displayed on the vertical ruler when the insertion point is inside a table. You can click and drag these to adjust the height of a row. When you adjust a row height in this way it adopts the **At Least** height option.

——— 7.4 Inserting and deleting ———

When working with your table, you may find that you need to insert (or delete) rows or columns.

The Insert Table tool on the Standard toolbar plays an interesting role in this area – watch how it changes its function!

To insert a row:

1 Position the insertion point within the row that will be below the row you are about to insert. If you want to add more than one row, select the number of rows required (see page 100) – that number of new rows will be inserted

2 Click the **Insert Rows** tool ![icon] on the Standard toolbar

To insert a column within a table:

1 Select the column that will be to the right of the new column you are about to insert. If you want to add more than one column, select the number of columns required (see page 100) – that number of new columns will be inserted

2 Click the **Insert Columns** tool ![icon] on the Standard toolbar

You may find that you have to adjust the width of your columns to accommodate the new columns you add.

To insert a column to the right of a table:

1 Show your non-printing characters if necessary ![icon]

2 Select the column outside the last border or gridline (the sunshine characters that mark the ends of the rows)

3 Click the **Insert Columns** tool ![icon] on the Standard toolbar

To delete a row:

1 Select the row (or rows) that you want to delete

2 Open the **Table** menu and choose **Delete Rows**

To delete a column:

1 Select the column (or columns) that you want to delete

2 Open the **Table** menu and choose **Delete Columns**

To delete an entire table:

1 Open the **Table** menu and choose **Select Table**

2 Open the **Table** menu and choose **Delete Rows**

If you press the **[Delete]** key on your keyboard, the contents of the table are deleted, but the table remains in place.

Row inserted   ↓

CONTACT	ADDRESS	NOTES	COST
Jill Syme	Old Mill Inn 24 Mill Lane Melrose	Delightful retreat in the Scottish borders. Food from 10 am until 10 pm. Excellent lunches and evening meal. Accommodation available. Working waterwheel, herb garden and riverside walks.	Lunches from £4 Dinner from £11.50 Dinner, Bed and Breakfast:£35
Kathy or Anna	Kathy's Kitchen 12 High Street Duns	Excellent family run coffee shop. Soup, baked potatoes, sandwiches etc all day. Delicious home baking!	Various.

↑ **Column inserted**

You may want to insert a cell (or cells) rather that a whole row or column. The technique is very similar.

1 Select the cell (or cells) that is currently where you want to insert a cell

2 Click the **Insert Cells** tool 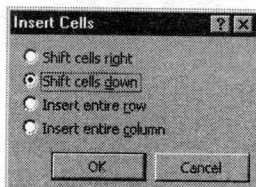 on the Standard toolbar

3 Complete the **Insert Cells** dialog box as required

4 Click **OK**

You can also delete cells in a similar way.

1 Select the cell (or cells) that you want to delete

2 Open the **Table** menu and choose **Delete Cells...**

3 Complete the **Delete Cells** dialog box as required

4 Click **OK**

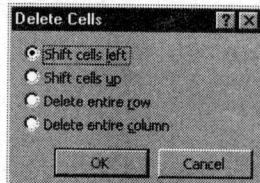

————————7.5 Merge and split cells————————

There will be times when you need to merge cells to achieve the effect you want within your table. For example, if you want to insert a heading that spans several columns you will need to merge several cells together in the heading row.

To merge cells:

1 Select the cells you want to merge
2 Choose **Merge Cells** from the **Table** menu
• The selected cells will combine to become one cell

CELLS MERGED HORIZONTALLY		
Cells merged vertically - across 3 rows and 1 column		
	Cells merged horizontally and vertically - across 2 columns and 3 rows	

You may also find that you need to split cells to get the effect you require in your table. There are variations on a theme when it comes to splitting cells – experiment with this until you get the hang of how it works.

To split cells:

1 Select the cells you want to split
2 Choose **Split Cells** from the **Table** menu
3 Complete the dialog box as required
4 Click **OK**

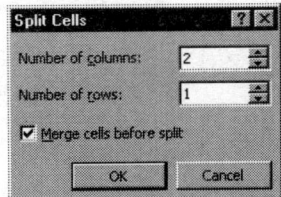

Split Cells   ? X

Number of columns: 2

Number of rows: 1

☑ Merge cells before split

     OK   Cancel

Two cells selected and split into 4 columns and
1 row, with **Merge cells before split** selected

CELLS MERGED HORIZONTALLY

One cell split into 3 columns
and 2 rows – **Merge cells
before split** is not relevant here

Two cells selected and split into
4 columns and 1 row, with **Merge
cells before split** *de*selected

As you can see, you could design some pretty complicated forms
by utilising the merge and split cell features.

RE-SIZING YOUR TABLE

If you create a table, e.g. 3 columns by 6 rows, then discover
you should have made it 4 columns by 6 rows, select the whole
table, then use **Split Cells** and specify the number of columns
and rows required. Leave the **Merge cells before split** checkbox
selected.

——————— 7.6 Drawing tables ———————

You may prefer to draw your tables onto your page. You can draw a table and make rows and columns very easily in Word.

To draw a table:

1 Display the **Tables and Borders** toolbar – click the **Tables and Borders** tool 🔲 on the Standard toolbar
2 The **Draw Table** tool is automatically selected (if you had the Tables and Borders toolbar displayed already, click the **Draw Table** tool 🖉 to select it)
3 Click and drag on your page to draw a rectangle the size you want your table to be
4 Draw in rows and columns where you want them
5 Switch the **Draw Table** tool off when you've finished – click 🖉 or press **[Esc]**

If you draw a line in the wrong place, remove it with the eraser.

1 Select the **Eraser** tool 🖉
2 Click and drag on the line you want to remove
3 Press **[Esc]** to cancel the Eraser tool, or click 🖉 again

If you want your rows or columns to be the same height or width, it can be a bit tricky when drawing a table. Use the **Cell Height and Width** dialog box to even things up – or use the **Distribute Rows Evenly** or **Distribute Columns Evenly** commands.

To distribute the row height evenly:

1 Select the rows you want to equalise

2 Click the **Distribute Rows Evenly** tool 🔳

To distribute the column width evenly:

1 Select the columns you want to equalise

2 Click the **Distribute Columns Evenly** tool 🔳

Any of the normal table handling features can by utilised in a table that you have drawn.

If you work with tables regularly you might want to show the Tables and Borders toolbar (even if you don't draw your table). It gives you shortcuts to many of the options you will use when working with tables.

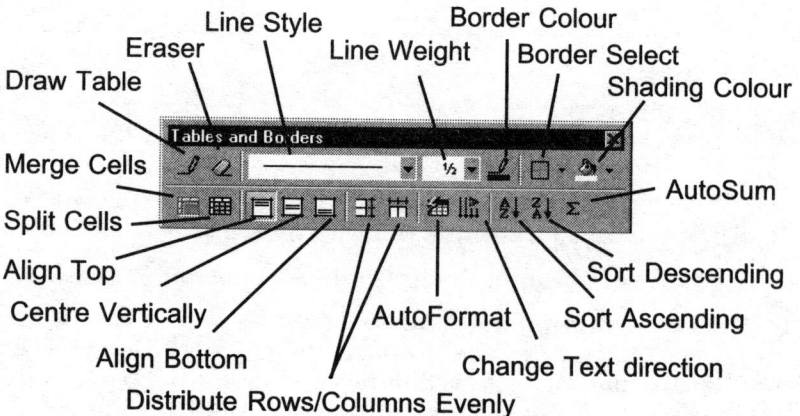

Experiment with the tools to see the effect they have on your data.

Book Sales (no of books) 1st Quarter 1997			
	January	February	March
Children's	500	650	543
Adult Fiction	450	430	654

The table above has the text and data:
• Centred vertically in each cell.
• Centred horizontally in each cell.
• Has the Colorful 1 Table Autoformat applied to it.

——————7.7 Sorting data in tables——————

Tables are often used to produce a list of data – names and phone numbers, stock items, student names, etc.

Lists of data often need to be manipulated and sorted into different orders – this is easily done in a table.

The list in the table below could be sorted in a number of ways:
• On a single column, e.g. Country order or Town order.
• An alphabetical listing on Surname then Firstname order.
• A listing in Country order, and then in Town order.
• A listing in Country, Town then Surname order.
You can sort on up to 3 levels at a time.

Firstname	Surname	Address	Town	Country
Jill	Wilson	22 High Street	Birmingham	England
Robert	Adamson	4a Mill Wynd	Greenlaw	Scotland
Malcolm	Simpson	West Wind Cottage	Perth	Scotland
Alison	Birch	10 High Croft	Birmingham	England
William	Smith	14 Hill Rise	Ascot	England
Carol	Adamson	Summerfield Way	Perth	Scotland
Rebecca	Jackson	102 Lower Lane	Cardiff	Wales
Gordon	Peterson	13 Grange Loan	Edinburgh	Scotland
Penny	Fullerton	82 All Saints Way	Cork	Ireland
James	Russell	2a Ferry Lane	Ascot	England

To perform a simple sort, on one column:

1 Place the insertion point inside the column you want to sort

2 Click the **Sort Ascending** 🔼 or the **Sort Descending** 🔽 tool on the Tables and Borders toolbar

To sort the list on Surname then Firstname order:

1 Position the insertion point anywhere within the table

2 Open the **Table** menu and choose **Sort...**

3 Complete the dialog box as required – in this example we have selected **Sort by** *Surname*, **Then by** *Firstname*, and both are **Ascending**.

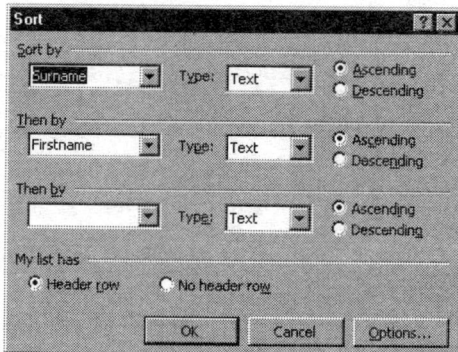

4 Click **OK**

Note that:

- You can sort in ascending or descending order.

- Different types of data can be sorted – Text, Number or Date.

- The table may or may not have a Header Row. The Header Row is the first row in your table – it usually contains column headings. If the first row is to be sorted along with the other rows, select the **No header row** button.

The result is displayed in the table below.

Firstname	Surname	Address	Town	Country
Carol	Adamson	Summerfield Way	Perth	Scotland
Robert	Adamson	4a Mill Wynd	Greenlaw	Scotland
Alison	Birch	10 High Croft	Birmingham	England
Penny	Fullerton	82 All Saints Way	Cork	Ireland
Rebecca	Jackson	102 Lower Lane	Cardiff	Wales
Gordon	Peterson	13 Grange Loan	Edinburgh	Scotland
James	Russell	2a Ferry Lane	Ascot	England
Malcolm	Simpson	West Wind Cottage	Perth	Scotland
William	Smith	14 Hill Rise	Ascot	England
Jill	Wilson	22 High Street	Birmingham	England

──────── 7.8 Simple sums ────────

It is possible to do some calculations in your table. If you use Excel as well as Word, it's often easier to insert an Excel worksheet as an object in your document (see Chapter 14), and use Excel's functions to work on your figures. However, it you do want to do calculations in Word, here's how!

Put the insertion point in the cell you want to contain a formula.

1 Open the **Table** menu and choose **Formula...**

2 If the Formula suggested is not the one you want, delete it and enter the formula required

3 If you want to specify a number format, e.g. *Currency*, select it from the **Number Format:** list

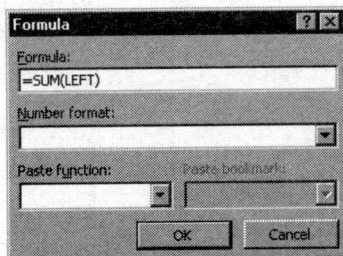

4 Click **OK**

Formula	? ☒
Formula:	
=SUM(LEFT)	
Number format:	
	▼
Paste function:	Paste bookmark:
▼	▼
	OK	Cancel

Sales Figures (in £s)			
	JAN	FEB	MAR	TOTAL
Bill	12,300	10,500	9,750	32,550
Ann	14,320	12,300	10,650	37,270
Bert	10,430	8,450	12,500	31,380
TOTAL	37,050	31,250	32,900	101,200

The Formulae are entered as Fields in your table.

- The **AutoSum** tool ∑ on the Tables and Borders toolbar inserts the formula **=Sum (above)** or **=Sum (left)** in the cell that the insertion point is in.

If you change any of the figures in the cells that feed your formulae, the result is not updated automatically.

Some of the figures have been changed in the table below, but

Sales Figures (in £s)			
	JAN	FEB	MAR	TOTAL
Bill	*19,300*	10,500	9,750	32,550
Ann	14,320	*22,300*	*19,650*	37,270
Bert	*50,430*	*18,450*	12,500	31,380
TOTAL	37,050	31,250	32,900	101,200

the total row and column remain unchanged.

To update the cells with formulae in:

1 Select the entire table

Sales Figures (in £s)			
	JAN	FEB	MAR	TOTAL
Bill	19,300	10,500	9,750	*39,550*
Ann	14,320	22,300	19,650	*56,270*
Bert	50,430	18,450	12,500	*81,380*
TOTAL	*84,050*	*51,250*	*41,900*	*177,200*

2 Press [F9]

- The Formula fields are updated

Acceptable formulae include:

=Sum (above)
=Sum (left)
=A7+B6
=A1-B2
=A3/B6
=A4*B4
=Sum (A1: A6)
=Min (A3, A7, A11)
=Count (B7: B14)

Check out **Formulas** in the on-line help for more information.

7.9 Summary

This chapter has introduced tables – a very powerful and flexible feature in Word. We have discussed:

- Creating a table using the Insert Table method.
- Entering text and data into a table.
- Selection techniques within a table.
- Changing column widths and row heights.
- Editing the table structure by adding and deleting rows and columns, merging and splitting cells.
- Creating a table using the Draw method.
- Sorting data in tables.
- Simple calculations within tables.

8

MULTI-PAGE DOCUMENTS

8.1 Aims of this chapter

In this chapter we will consider some of the features that are useful when working with multi-page documents. Page breaks, moving through a long document, bookmarks, page numbering and headers and footers will be discussed. You will be introduced to Online Layout, Outline and Master Document view and will learn how to create a table of contents and an index.

8.2 Controlling page breaks

Controlling automatic page breaks

Automatic page breaks are inserted when your text reaches the end of a page. By default Word takes care of Widows and Orphans for you.

- A *widow* is the last line of a paragraph printed by itself at the top of a page.

- An *orphan* is the first line of a paragraph printed by itself at the bottom of a page.

You can switch the Widow/Orphan control and other pagination options on and off in the Format Paragraph dialog box:

1 Open the **Format** menu and choose **Paragraph**
2 Select the **Line and Page Breaks** tab
3 Select or deselect the Pagination options as required
4 Click **OK**

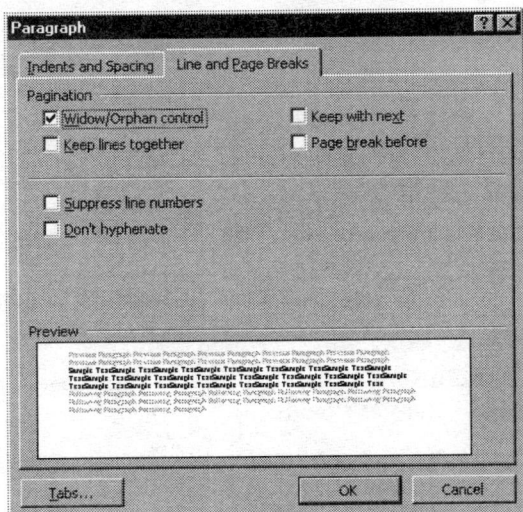

PAGINATION OPTIONS

Widow/Orphan control

Prevents Word from printing the first line of a paragraph at the bottom, or the last line of a paragraph at the top of a page.

Keep lines together

Prevents a page break within a paragraph.

Keep with next

Prevents a page break between the selected paragraph and the following one.

Page break before

Inserts a manual page break before the selected paragraph.

In Normal view a dotted line appear across your screen when an automatic page break occurs.

```

....................................................................................................................................

```

In Page Layout view, the insertion point moves to the top of the next page when an automatic page break occurs.

MANUAL PAGE BREAKS

You can force a page break before you fill a page with text, rather than wait for automatic pagination to occur if you need to.

To insert a manual page break:

• Hold down the **[Ctrl]** key and press **[Enter]**.

If you are in Normal view a dotted line will appear across your screen with the text *Page Break* in the middle of it.

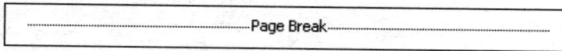

```

...................................................................Page Break................................

```

If you are in Page Layout view, the insertion point moves to the top of the next page.

• To remove a manual page break use either the **[Delete]** key (if the page break is to the right of the insertion point) or the **[←]** key (if the page break is to the left of the insertion point).

——— 8.3 Headers and footers ———

In multi-page documents Headers and Footers are often used. Each page has a header area in the top margin and a footer area in the bottom margin.

The headers and footers in your document don't have to be the same on each page.

You can choose from having the headers and footers:

- The same on every page (this is the default option).
- Different for the first page of your document.
- Different on odd and even pages.

To create a header and/or footer:

1 Open the **View** menu and choose **Header and Footer**

2 Type your header

3 Click the **Switch Between Header and Footer** tool ⬚ on the Header and Footer toolbar to move to the footer area and enter your footer text

4 Click **Close** on the Header and Footer toolbar when you've finished

The Header and Footer toolbar appears automatically when you view your Headers and Footers.

Notice that there are two tabs set in the Header and Footer areas - a centre tab in the middle of the line, and a right tab at the right margin. Tab into these if you want to centre your header or footer, or align it to the right.

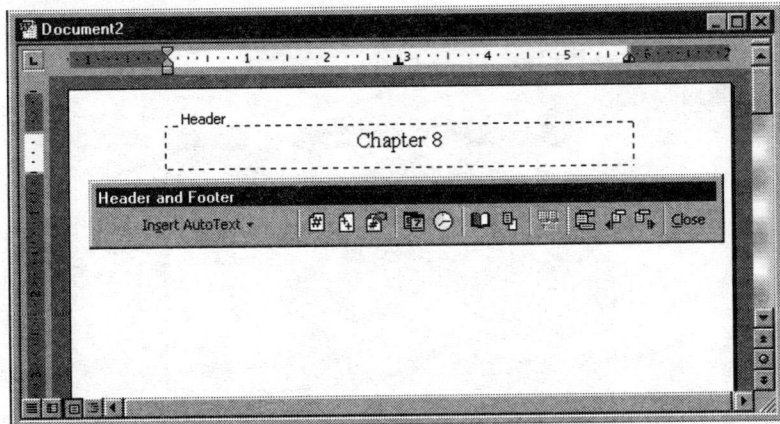

The Header and Footer toolbar contains useful tools for entering AutoText entries, page numbers, date, time, etc, and for changing your header and footer options.

PAGE NUMBERS

DO NOT type a number in the header or footer area to insert a page number – you will get whatever number you type repeated on every page!

Use the tools on the Header and Footer toolbar, or an AutoText entry, to create a page numbering field.

If you want to format your page number, or start numbering at a number other than 1, click the **Format Page Number** tool 🔐 and format as necessary.

If you want the header or footer on your first page to be different to the header or footer on the other pages in your document (in some cases you may not want any header or footer on the first page) you must go into the Page Setup dialog box.

1 Open the **View** menu and choose **Header and Footer**

2 Click the **Page Setup** tool 🔲 on the Header and Footer toolbar

3 Select the **Different first page** checkbox on the **Layout** tab in the Page Setup dialog box

4 Click **OK**

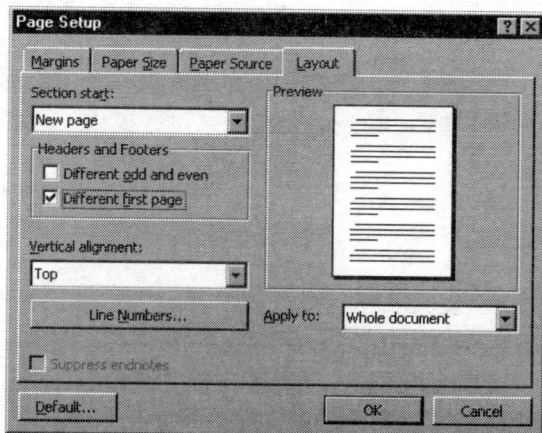

5 Use the **Show Previous** and **Show Next** tools to move between your first page header or footer area, and the header or footer area for the rest of the document.

6 Enter your header and footer detail as required

7 Click **Close** on the Header and Footer toolbar

Setting up a different header and footer for odd and even pages is done in a very similar way:

1 Open the **View** menu and choose **Header and Footer**

2 Click the **Page Setup** tool

3 Select the **Different odd and even** checkbox on the **Layout** tab

4 Click **OK**

5 Use the **Show Previous** and **Show Next** tool to move between the odd page header or footer area, and the even page header or footer area

6 Enter your header and footer detail as required

7 Click **Close** on the Header and Footer toolbar

• You can select both the **Different First Page** and the **Different odd and even** checkboxes if you wish.

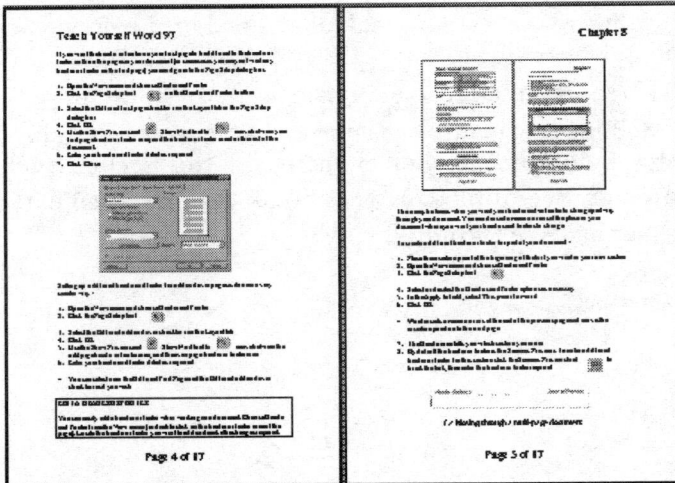

EDIT A HEADER OR FOOTER

You can easily edit a header or footer when working on a document. Choose Header and Footer from the View menu (or double click on the header or footer area of the page). Locate the header or footer you want to edit and make the changes required.

There may be times when you want your header and/or footer to change part way through your document. You must insert a section break at the place in your document where you want your headers and footers to change.

To create a different header or footer for part of your document:

1 Place the insertion point at the beginning of the text you want in your new section

2 Open the **View** menu and choose **Header and Footer**

3 Click the **Page Setup** tool

4 Select or deselect the Headers and Footer options as necessary

5 In the **Apply to** field, select **This point forward**

6 Click **OK**

• Word inserts a section break at the end of the previous page and moves the insertion point on to the next page.

7 The Header area tells you which section you are in

8 By default the header or footer is the **Same as Previous**. To enter a different header or footer for this section click the **Same as Previous** tool to break the link, then enter the header or footer required

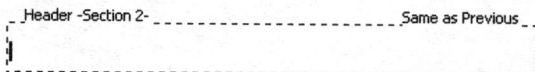

```
_ Header -Section 2- _ _ _ _ _ _ _ _ _ _ _ _ _ _ _ _ _ _ _ _ _ Same as Previous _ _
|                                                                              |
| I                                                                            |
'- - - - - - - - - - - - - - - - - - - - - - - - - - - - - - - - - - - - - - -'
```

— 8.4 Moving through a long document —

You probably use the scroll bars to move through your document most of the time. There are some other methods you might like to experiment with if you work with longer documents.

- Click and drag the scroll box on the vertical scrollbar – a prompt appears to tell you which page you're at. Let go the mouse button when you reach the one required.

- To go to the top of the previous page click the **Previous Page** button at the bottom of the vertical scroll bar.

- To go to the top of the next page click the **Next Page** button at the bottom of the vertical scroll bar.

To go to a specific page number:

1 Double click the page number indicator `Page 7` at the left end of the status bar

2 Enter the page number you want to go to

3 Click **Go To**

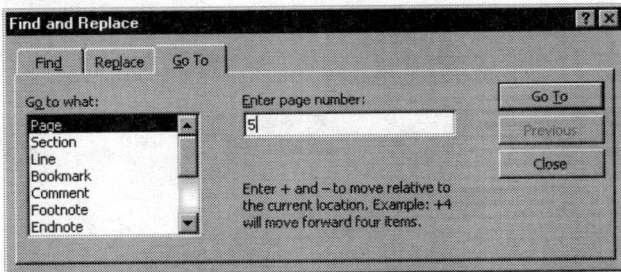

- Experiment with the other options in the **Go to what:** list and use any that are useful to you.

Bookmarks

There may be times when you know that you will want to be able to return to a specific place in your file quickly. You should insert a 'bookmark' to mark the spot, then you can jump to the bookmark easily whenever you need to.

To insert a bookmark:

1 Place the insertion point at the place you want to be able to jump to
2 Open the **Insert** menu and choose **Bookmark**
3 Give your bookmark a name
4 Click **Add**

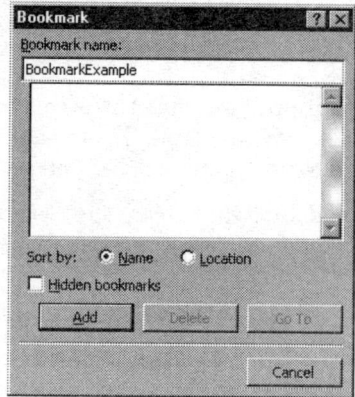

To jump to the bookmark:

1 Double click the page number indicator at the left end of the status bar
2 Choose **Bookmark** from the **Go to what:** list
3 Select your bookmark from the **Enter Bookmark Name** list
4 Click **Go To**

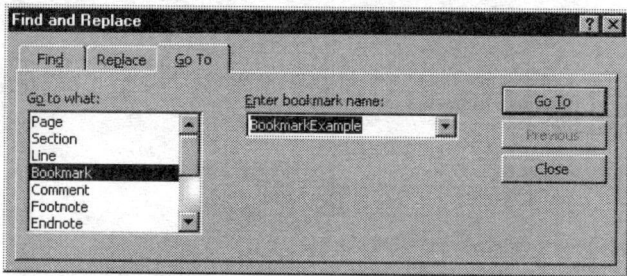

To delete a bookmark:

1 Open the **Insert** menu and choose **Bookmark**
2 Select the bookmark you want to delete
3 Click **Delete**
4 Close the **Bookmark** dialog box

8.5 Online Layout view

Online Layout view is a new option in Word 97, which aims to make it easier to read documents online. It can be a very useful view when working on a long document.

To view your document in Online Layout view:

- Click the **Online Layout** view tool 🔲

Your document is displayed at the right side of the screen, and the Document Map, displaying the outline structure of your document, is displayed down the left side of the screen.

The document text appears larger, and wraps to fit the window rather than appear as it will print.

You can edit your document as usual in the document window.

Document Map

You can use the Document Map to move quickly from one part of your document to another – simply click on the heading you want to move to.

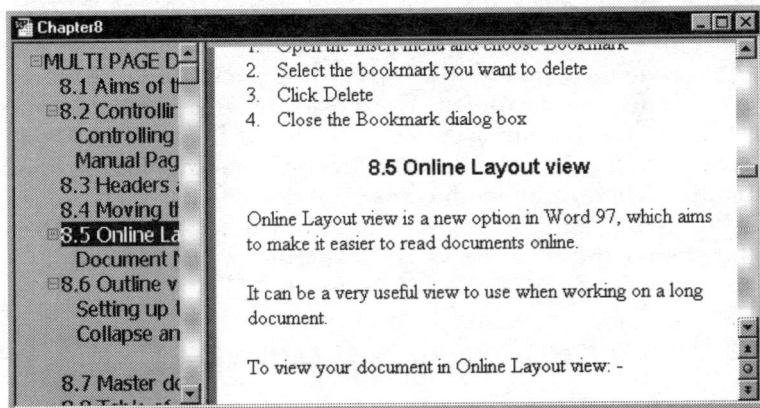

The map is made up of all text formatted with a Heading style

The Document Map pane can be resized by clicking and dragging its right-most edge – a Resize prompt appears when the mouse pointer is in the correct place.

The Document Map is displayed automatically when you go into Online Layout view, but it can be displayed in any view – click the Document Map tool 🔍 on the Standard toolbar to toggle it on and off.

To return to any other view from Online Layout view:

• Open the **View** menu and select the view required.

———— 8.6 Outline view ————

If you create long, structured documents – reports, minutes, thesis, etc – Outline view is worth experimenting with.

Outline view is useful when you want to look at the structure of your document in terms of main headings, subheadings, etc.

It is often a good idea to go into Outline view and type in the structure of your document, then return to Normal or Page Layout view to enter the bulk of your text.

Alternatively, enter your text in Normal or Page Layout view, using the Word Heading 1 to Heading 9 styles to format the headings in your document. Word uses these styles to determine the structure of your document when you take it into Outline view. Heading 1 is the highest level of heading you can have, Heading 9 is the lowest one. For most documents you'll probably use no more than four heading levels. Change to Outline view when you want view or edit the structure of your file.

Setting up the structure in Outline view

1 Create a new document

2 Click the **Outline View** tool 🔲 to go into Outline view

3 Type in the headings and sub-headings for your document – they are automatically formatted using the Heading 1 style

Outline view has its own toolbar to help you work on the structure of your document.

Demote and **Promote** the headings as necessary to get the structure required.

If you want to type in some body text (not a heading, but text formatted using the Normal style) in Outline view, click the **Demote to Body Text** tool then enter your text.

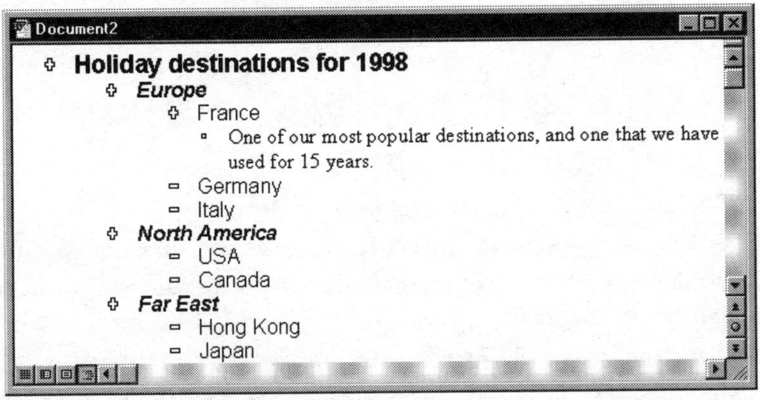
Document2
Holiday destinations for 1998
Europe
France
One of our most popular destinations, and one that we have used for 15 years.
Germany
Italy
North America
USA
Canada
Far East
Hong Kong
Japan

You will notice ✚ and ▭ signs down the left-hand side of your headings in Outline view. ✚ means that the heading has either sub-headings or body text under it, ▭ means that there is nothing at a lower level. Body text has ▫ to the left of it.

Collapse and expand

There may be times when you don't want to display the entire document in Outline view. You might want to view only the Heading 1 level paragraphs or your headings from Heading 1 to Heading 2 level only.

In Outline view you can collapse or expand your documents to show just the level of detail required.

To collapse the whole document to a given level:

• Click the appropriate **Show Heading** tool on the Outlining toolbar

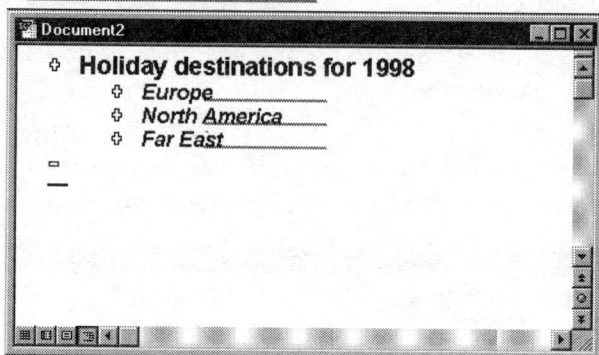

You can rearrange the structure of your document by moving large chunks of text very quickly in Outline view – much quicker than a cut and paste manoeuvre would allow.

To expand the whole document again:

• Click the **Show All Headings** tool

To collapse or expand individual areas in your document:

1 Place the insertion point inside the heading that you want to expand or collapse

2 Click the **Expand** or **Collapse** tool as required

To display only the first line of paragraphs at the body text level

• Click the **Show First Line Only** tool

You can rearrange the structure of your document by moving large chunks of text very quickly in Outline view – much quicker than a cut and paste manoeuvre would allow.

To rearrange the structure or your document:

1 Collapse or expand the outline until you can see the heading you want to move. If you want to move its substructure with it, collapse the substructure, so you can just see the heading

2 Select the heading – place the insertion point within it

3 Click the **Move Up** or **Move Down** tool until the paragraph is in its new position

Any substructure the heading has will be moved with it.

——— 8.7 Master Document view ———

A Master Document is a container for other documents. It is a useful option for very long documents – long manuals or books – where you may have several files (perhaps one for each section of a manual, or chapter of a book) making up your final document.

By collecting the files together into a Master Document, page numbering, headers and footers, table of contents and indexes can be generated more easily across all the subdocuments.

When you collect your subdocuments into a Master Document, you have quick and easy access to each subdocument without having to continually open and close individual files.

You can either:

• Create your subdocuments from within a Master Document.

Or

• Insert existing documents into your Master Document.

To create your subdocuments within a Master Document:

1 Create a new file to be your Master Document

2 Open the **View** menu and choose **Master Document**

3 Key in an Outline for your document (see 8.6 above)

4 Select the headings and text you want to separate into subdocuments

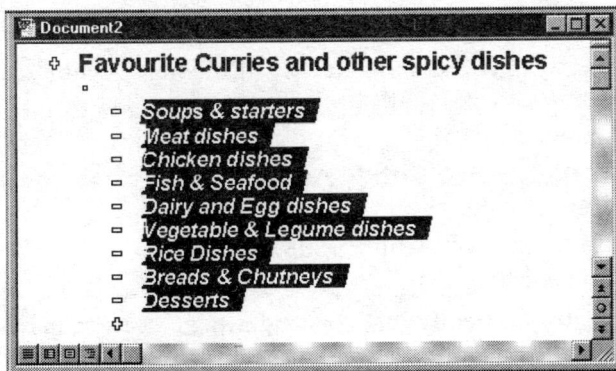

- Ensure that the first heading you select is formatted with the heading style you want to use for each subdocument. For example, if the heading for each subdocument is formatted using Heading 2, make sure that this is the level of the first text within your selection. Word will then create a new subdocument each time it finds a Heading 2 style.

5 Click the **Create Subdocument tool** 🖹 on the Master Document toolbar

6 Save your Master Document

- Word will automatically save each subdocument, with the subdocumentss headings used for the file names.

- Word automatically inserts a continuous section break above and below each subdocument when you create them this way.

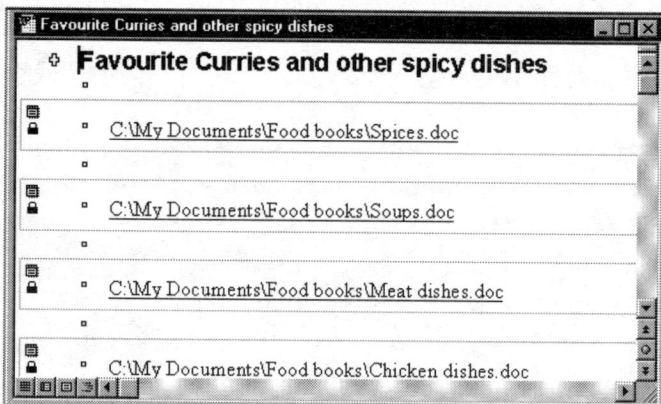

To insert existing documents into your Master Document:

1 Display your Master Document in Master Document view

2 Position the insertion point where you want to insert your document

3 Click the **Insert Subdocument** tool 🖺 on the Master Document toolbar

4 Locate the file you want to insert

5 Click Open

- Word automatically inserts a next page section break above and a continuous section break below the inserted document.

When you open a Master Document the subdocuments are collapsed. Click the **Expand Subdocuments** tool 🔂 on the Master Document toolbar to expand them.

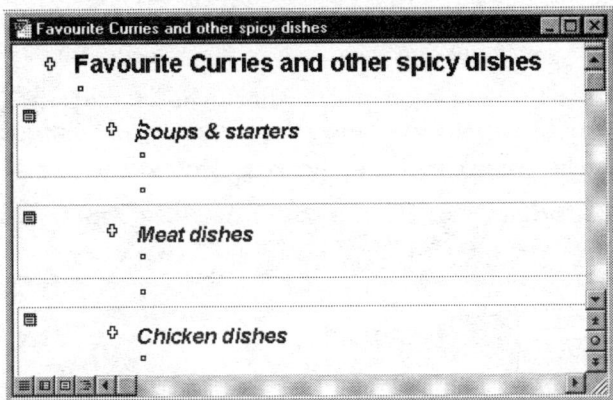

To open your subdocuments from the Master Document:

- If the subdocuments are collapsed, click on the name of the subdocument you want to open.
- If the subdocuments are expanded, double click on the subdocument icon to the left of the subdocument heading.

When the subdocuments are expanded, you can use the Outlining toolbar to control the amount of detail displayed in your Master Document (see expanding and collapsing the outline in 8.6 above).

To print your Master Document:

1 Expand the subdocuments in Master Document view
2 Go into Normal view
3 Print as usual

If you don't want to print all of the subdocument:

1 Expand the subdocuments in Master Document view
2 Collapse or expand each document to display the level of detail required
3 Open the **File** menu and choose **Print**
4 Specify the options required and click **OK**

——8.8 Table of contents (TOC)——

You can create a TOC for your document very quickly, provided
that you have used the built-in heading styles Heading 1 to
Heading 9 to format the headings in your document.

1 Position the insertion point where you want your Table of
Contents – usually at or near the beginning of your document.

2 Open the **Insert** menu and choose **Index and Tables**

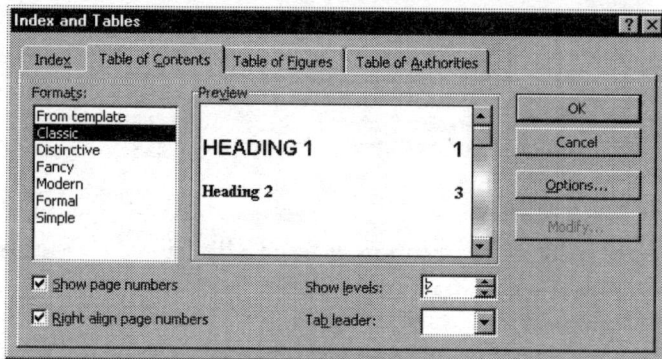

3 On the **Table of Contents** tab select the number of **Show
levels** and **Tab leader** if required

4 Click **OK**

8.1 Aims of this chapter 1

8.2 Controlling page breaks 1

8.3 Headers and footers 3

8.4 Moving through a multi-page document......6

8.5 Online Layout view...8

8.6 Outline view..10

8.7 Master document view...................................12

8.8 Table of contents (TOC)...............................14

8.9 Index..16

8.10 Summary...17

You can still get Word to generate a table of contents automatically, even if you haven't formatted your entries using the Heading 1 to Heading 9 styles.

You must enter *TC field codes* into your document to indicate where your tables of contents entries are taken from. Then you generate your TOC using these field codes.

1 Position the insertion point immediately in front of the text you are generating a TOC code for

2 Open the **Insert** menu and choose **Field...**

3 Choose **Index and Tables** in the **Categories** list

4 Select **TC** in the **Field names:** list

5 Type the text you want to appear in the TOC in the **Field codes:** area

• DO NOT remove the TC code from the entry

6 Click **OK**

Field ? X

Categories:

(All)
Date and Time
Document Automation
Document Information
Equations and Formulas
Index and Tables
Links and References
Mail Merge
Numbering
User Information

Field names:

Index
RD
TA
TC
TOA
TOC
XE

Field codes: TC "Text" [Switches]

TC "Holidays for children"

Description
Mark a table of contents entry

☐ Preserve formatting during updates

OK   Cancel   Options...

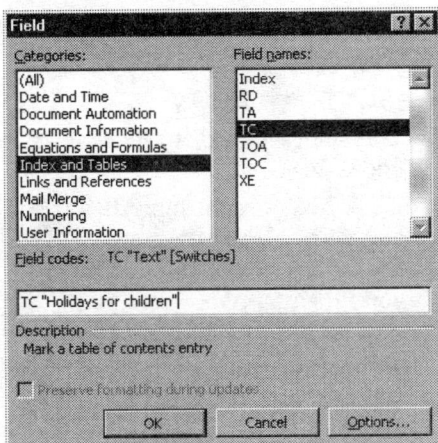

To generate a TOC using Field Codes:

1 Position the insertion point where you want your Table of Contents to appear

2 Open the **Insert** menu and choose **Index and Tables**

3 Select the **Table of Contents** tab

4 Click **Options...**

5 Select the **Table entry fields** checkbox and click **OK**

6. Click **OK** again at the Index and Tables dialog box

• To quickly get to a page in your document, click the page number you want to jump to on your Table of Contents page.

8.9 Index

If your document needs an index, you can get Word to automate this process too.

There are two steps to generating an index:

• Marking the entries you want to appear in the index.
• Creating the index.

To mark an index entry:

1 Select the word(s) you want to appear in your index
2 Open the **Insert** menu and choose **Index and Tables**
3 Select the **Index** tab
4 Click **Mark Entry**
5 The selected text appears in the **Main entry** field – edit it if necessary
6 Click **Mark** or **Mark All** if you want all occurrences of the same text marked in your document
7 The **Mark Index Entry** dialog box remains open so you can work through your document marking multiple entries
8 Click **Close** when you've finished

To create the index:

1 Place the insertion point where you want the index to appear – usually at the end of your file
2 Open the **Insert** menu and choose **Index and Tables**
3 Select the **Index** tab
4 Specify the options required for your index
5 Click **OK**

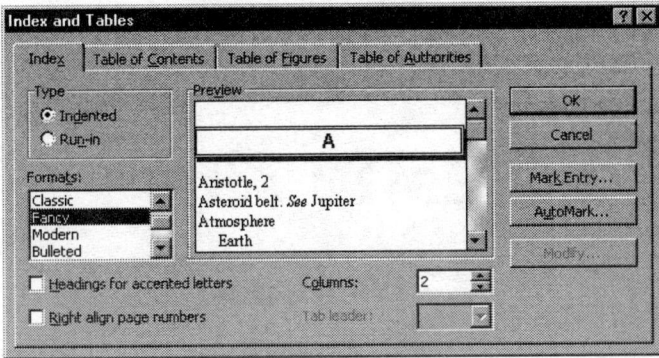

8.10 Summary

In this chapter we have discussed features that are particularly useful when you work with long documents. You have learnt about:

- Automatic and manual page breaks.
- Headers and footers.
- Page numbering.
- Moving through multi-page documents.
- Inserting and using a Bookmark
- Online Layout view.
- Outline view.
- Master Document view.
- Creating a table of contents.
- Creating an index.

9

TEMPLATES

9.1 Aims of this chapter

This chapter discusses templates - the patterns on which all your documents are based. So far, we have used the Blank Document template for most of our documents, and have had a look at some of the document wizards available (which are a bit like interactive templates) in Chapter 5. In this chapter, we will look at some of the other templates that come with Word, set up templates from scratch and design an on-line form.

9.2 Word templates

To create new documents using the Blank Document template you simply click the New tool on the Standard toolbar. The document created has an A4 paper size, 1" top and bottom margin, 1.25" left and right margin and single line spacing. Paragraph and character styles that are part of the Blank Document template are available in the style list on the Formatting toolbar.

Word comes with several other templates ready for you to use. You should look through these templates as you may find some of them useful. Included in the templates are several letter, memo, fax, and résumé (CV) templates to choose from. If you find a template you would like to use, you can customise it with your own company details, etc, and save it for future use.

To create a document using a Word template (other than the Blank Document template):

1 Open the **File** menu and choose **New**
2 Select a tab to display the templates available in each category (the Blank Document template is on the General tab)
3 Choose a template (not a *wizard* – see Chapter 5 if you need help with the wizard templates)
4 Click **OK**

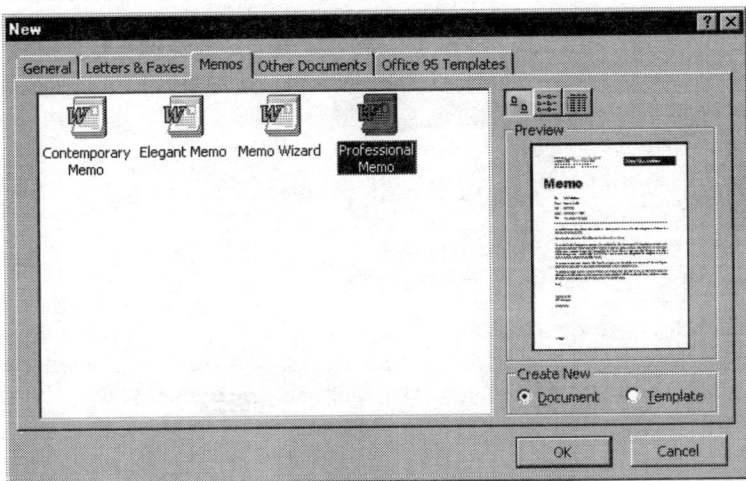

Explore the document that you have created. Check out the layout – notice that some templates, e.g. memo, fax, include areas for your company name, address, telephone/fax number, etc.

Many of the documents created using a Word template include details on how to use and complete the document that you have created.

```
                                    ┌──────────────────────────┐
                                    │  Company Name Here        │
                                    └──────────────────────────┘

    Memo

         To     [Click here and type name]
         From:  [Click here and type name]
         CC:    [Click here and type name]
         Date:  14/07/97
         Re:    [Click here and type subject]


         How to Use This Memo Template

         Select text you would like to replace, and type your memo. Use styles such as Heading 1-3 and
         Body text in the Style control on the Formatting toolbar. To save changes to this template for future
         use, choose Save As from the File menu. In the Save As Type box, choose Document Template.
         Next time you want to use it, choose New from the File menu, and then double-click your template.
```

In the main, you just follow the instructions on the screen. Select
and replace pieces of text that are used to prompt you for your
own details e.g. **Company Name Here**

With other prompts, e.g. **[Click here and type name]** just do
as you're told – click in the highlighted area and enter your
information. The highlighted area is actually a *Text Form Field*
– you'll learn how to set these up later (see 9.4 Creating your
own templates).

Check out the styles available in your document – click the drop-
down arrow to the right of the Style box on the Formatting
toolbar. You can edit these styles, or add to them if you wish (see
Chapter 6 for more information on styles).

—9.3 Customising the Word templates—

If you find a template that you would like to use, you should
customise it with your own company details and save the
customised template for future use.

If you don't customise it, you will need to enter standard information, your company name, address, phone number, etc, on every document that you create using the original template. By writing your own information into a template, your details will appear automatically on each new document.

You can customise *any* part of a template – not just the company detail areas. Page layout, headers, footers, styles, etc, can all be modified to suit your requirements.

To customise your template:

1   Create a new document using the template you wish to customise

2   Customise your document as required – enter you own company name, address, etc.

3   Open the **File** menu and choose **Save As...**

4   In the **Save as type** field, choose **Document Template**

5   Select the folder in which you wish to store your template – choose either the Templates folder or one of its subfolders

6   Give your template a name

•   To replace the original template with your customised one, save your template in the same folder as the original template and use the original template name.

•   To keep the original template and save your customised one separately, use a different name.

7   Click **Save**

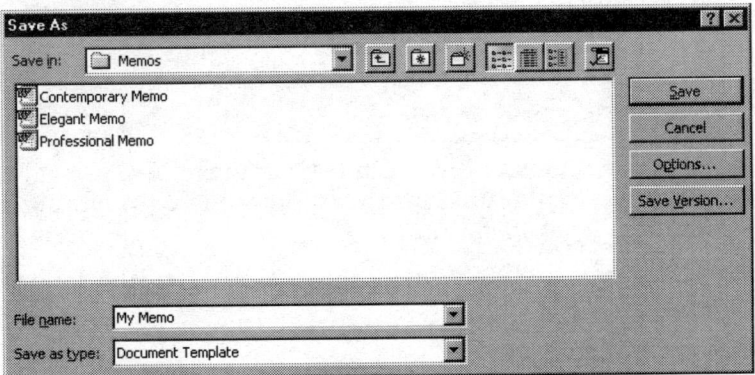

—— 9.4 Creating your own templates ——

You can easily create your own templates to look like the letters, memos, faxes and forms you currently use.

To create your own template:

1 Open the **File** menu and choose **New**
2 Choose the template that you want to base your new template on – probably the *Blank Document* template on the **General** tab
3 Select **Template** from the **Create New** options
4 Click **OK**

A new template – with its temporary filename *Template1* displayed in the title bar – is created.

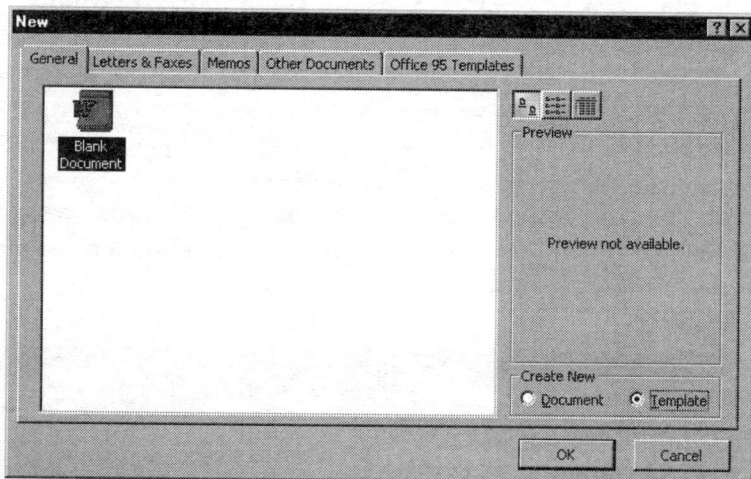

Design your template – you can set margins, line spacing, add or edit styles, enter standard text, etc – in fact anything you would do in a document file.

Try designing a simple memo form similar to the following example.

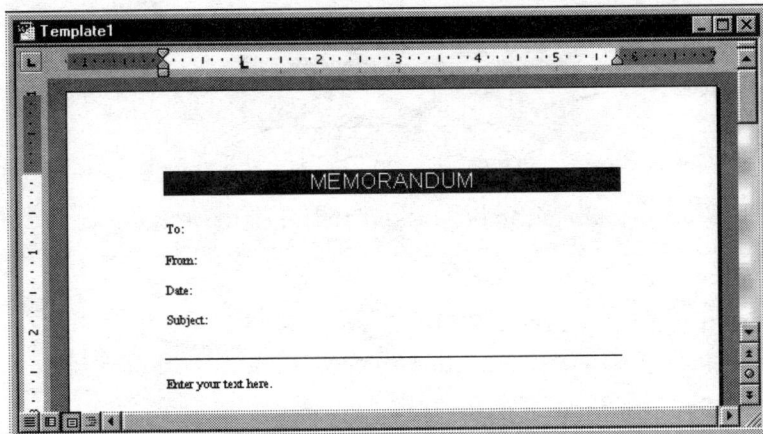

![Screenshot of a Word template window titled "Template1" showing a MEMORANDUM form with To:, From:, Date:, and Subject: prompts, and the text "Enter your text here."]

Form Fields

To make your template easier to use, you can add special *Form Fields* to it.

The **To:**, **From:** and **Subject:** prompts could be followed by *Text Form Fields* – so you can just click in them and key in your detail. You could also add a Text Form Field to automatically display the current date after the **Date:** prompt.

The Forms Toolbar is used to add form fields to your file.

To display the Forms toolbar:

1 Point to any toolbar that is displayed and click the right mouse button

2 Left click on Forms

or

1 Open the **View** menu and choose **Toolbars**

2 Left click on the toolbar you wish to display

You can hide or show any toolbar at anytime using either of the above techniques – the commands toggle the display of the toolbars on and off. (For more information on toolbars see Chapter 13).

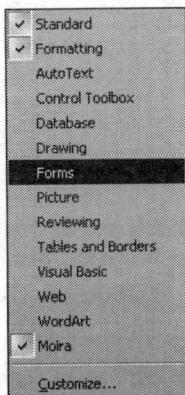

Menu list:
- ✓ Standard
- ✓ Formatting
- AutoText
- Control Toolbox
- Database
- Drawing
- **Forms**
- Picture
- Reviewing
- Tables and Borders
- Visual Basic
- Web
- WordArt
- ✓ Moira
- Customize...

Drop-Down list   Draw Table   Insert Frame

Text ———————

——— Protect Form

Check Box   Options   Insert Table   Form Field Shading

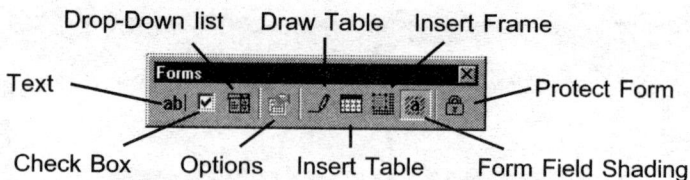

The Forms toolbar can be 'docked' to the right, left, top or bottom of the screen – drag and drop its Title Bar to position the toolbar where you wish.

To add a Text Form Field to your file:

1 Place the insertion point where you want the Form Field

2 Click the **Text Form Field** tool [abl]

The Form Field will probably appear shaded, so you can see where it is. If it doesn't, click the **Form Field Shading** tool [a] to switch the shading on.

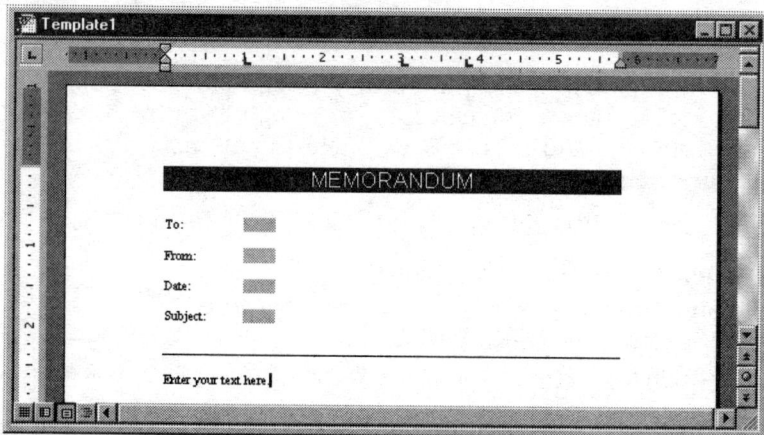

To add prompts to the Text Form Fields:

1. Double click on the Text Form Field

or

Select the **Text Form Field** (click on it) and click the **Form Field Options** tool [🗐]

2 Enter the prompt in the **Default text:** field

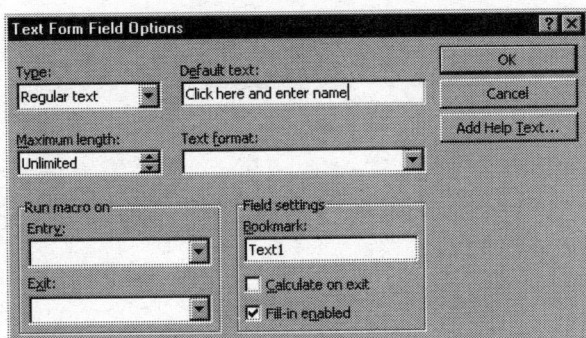

3 Click **OK**

Add prompts to each field as required.

To get the date Text Form Field to complete automatically:

1 Create a **Text Form Field** after the *Date:* label
2 Double click on the **Text Form Field**

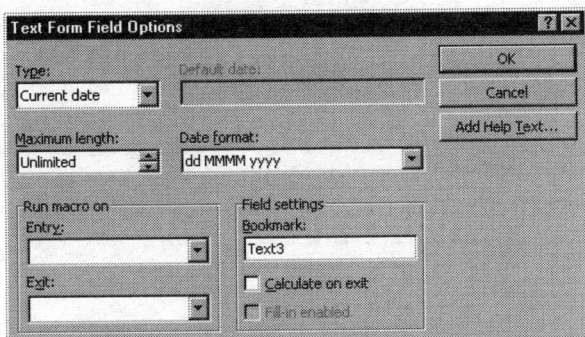

3 Choose **Current date** from the **Type:** list
4 Select a date format from the **Date format:** list
5 Click **OK**

Modify or complete your template as required, e.g. add page numbering to the page footer and then save your template.

To save your template:

1 Click the **Save** tool on the Standard toolbar
2 Select the folder you want to store your template in – the Templates folder or one of its subfolders

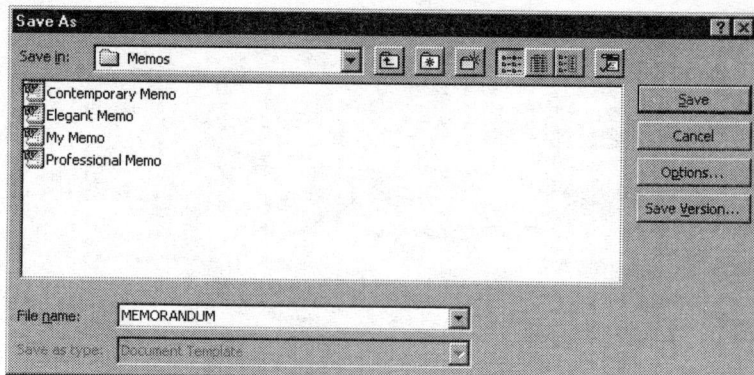

Save in: [ ] Memos ▼ [icons]

[icon] Contemporary Memo
[icon] Elegant Memo
[icon] My Memo
[icon] Professional Memo

Save
Cancel
Options...
Save Version...

File name: MEMORANDUM ▼
Save as type: Document Template ▼

3   Edit the file name if necessary

4   Click **Save**

5   Close your template

• You can now create memos using your own template any time
  you wish.

You can create templates for all the forms you use – order forms,
invoices, booking forms, etc.

Look through the Word templates to get some ideas – the **Office
95 Template** tab (choose **New** from the **File** menu to access the
New dialog box) gives examples of many different document
layouts, including Certificates, Brochures, Newsletters and
Directories.

9.5 Summary

In this chapter we have discussed templates – those that come
with Word and ones that you can create for yourself. You should
now know how to:

• Use the templates that come with Word.

• Customise the templates that come with Word.

• Create templates of your own.

10

MAIL MERGE

10.1 Aims of this chapter

This chapter discusses mail merge. Mail merge is used to produce customised standard letters, forms or mailing labels. You will learn how to set up main documents, data documents and how to combine the two to produce your 'result documents'. Selective merge will also be addressed. With selective merge you combine only the data records that match specific criteria with your main document. You will also find out how to produce mailing labels.

10.2 Mail merge terminology

Mail merge uses jargon and techniques that are similar to those found in database applications. You are actually performing very basic database routines when you use mail merge.

Terminology you will encounter:

- *Main document* – the document that contains the layout, standard text and field names that point to the data source.
- *Data source* – the file that contains the records you require

for your mail merge – perhaps a name and address file. The data source is usually in a table layout. It could be a Word file or a table in Access or Excel if you have them installed. Other data sources can be used – see the on-line Help for details. We will create our data source in Word.

- *Record* – a record contains all the information on each item in your data source.
- *Field* – a piece of data within a record. Title, surname, first name, telephone number, etc, would be held in separate fields.
- *Field name* – the name used to identify a field.
- *Result document* – the document produced when you combine the records in the data source with the main document.

There are three steps involved in mail merge:

1 Creating the main document
2 Creating and/or locating the data source
3 Merging the two to produce the result document

We'll work through each of these steps in this chapter.

It doesn't matter whether you create the main document or data source document first – but you must have both before you can produce a result document.

——— 10.3 Creating the data source ———

We'll create the data source first. The easiest way to create this in Word is through the Mail Merge Helper dialog box. However, you must indicate what document you intend to use as your main document before you can create or locate your data source.

1 Create a new document (or open an existing one that you want to use for your main document)
2 Open the **Tools** menu and choose **Mail Merge...**
3 Choose **Create**, then **Form Letters** at step 1 in the Mail Merge Helper dialog box

4 Select **Active Window** at the prompt

5 An **Edit** button now appears at step 1 – ignore this for the time being as we are going to create our data source

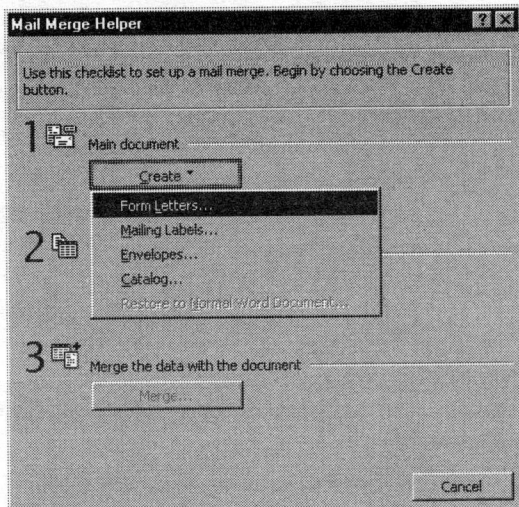

To create your data source file:

1 Click the **Get Data...** button at step 2

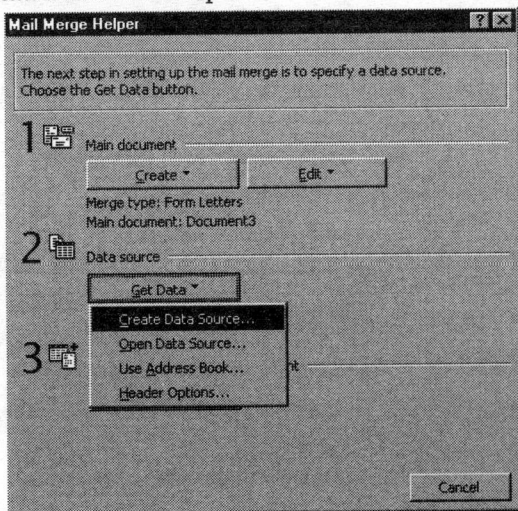

2 Choose **Create Data Source...**

- The **Create Data Source** dialog box appears.

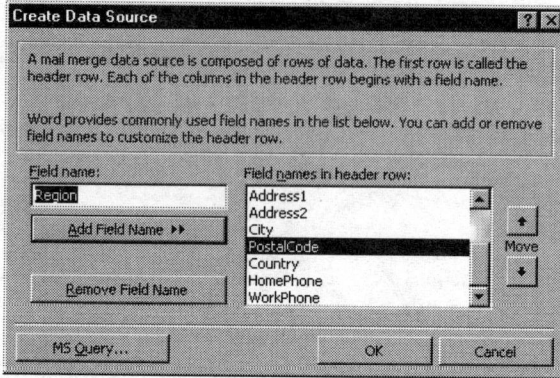

Word will eventually organise your data into rows in a table format. The first row of the table contains the field names and this row is called the *Header Row*.

Word automatically presents a list of the field names it suggests for the header row in your data source file.

1. Modify the header row list as required

- **To add a field name:**

  Enter the field name (single words only – no spaces) in the **Field name** slot and click the **Add Field Name** button

- **To remove a field name:**

  Select the field name from the **Field names in header row** list, and click the **Remove Field Name** button

- **To rearrange the order of the field names:**

  Select the field name you want to move in the **Field names in header row** list, and click the arrow buttons to the right of the list to move the field name up or down

2 Click **OK** once you've got the header row arranged as required

3 Give the file a suitable name at the **Save As** dialog box and click **Save**

4 Choose **Edit Data Source** to add your records

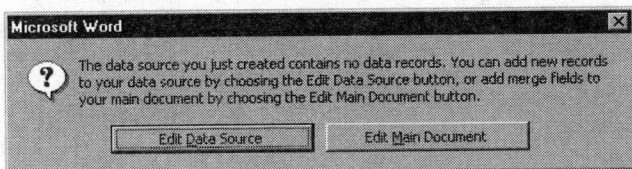

> **Microsoft Word** ☒
>
> (?) The data source you just created contains no data records. You can add new records to your data source by choosing the Edit Data Source button, or add merge fields to your main document by choosing the Edit Main Document button.
>
> [Edit Data Source]   [Edit Main Document]

To enter data:

1 Enter the data for the first record into the **Data Form**

* Press **[Tab]** to move from field to field.

2. Click **Add New** when you've completed one record and you want a new empty Data Form to complete

> **Data Form** [?][☒]
>
> | | | |
> |---|---|---|
> | Title: | Miss | OK |
> | FirstName: | Johanne | Add New |
> | LastName: | Andrews | Delete |
> | JobTitle: | Sales Manager | |
> | Company: | Andrews Design Ltd | Restore |
> | Address1: | Hilltop House | Find... |
> | Address2: | 44 Hill Street | |
> | Town: | GLASGOW | View Source |
> | Region: | Strathclyde | |
>
> Record: |◀ ◀ [1] ▶ ▶|

* Use the buttons at the bottom of the Data Form to move through your records to check them.

3 Click **View Source** when you've finished – this displays your data source file in a table layout

4 Save your file

DATA FORM AND DATA SOURCE

It is usually easier to add and edit records in your data source file using the Data Form – the table layout isn't as user-friendly. However, you must return to the source document to save your file – click the **View Source** button in the Data Form.

To display the Data Form again click the **Data Form** tool 🔳 on the Database toolbar.

10.4 Editing the data source

At some stage you will probably need to edit the records in your data file – perhaps change a contact name or a phone number.

The first thing you'll need to do is find the record you want to edit. You could do this using the buttons at the bottom left of the Data Form, but if your file contains many records it might be quicker to use **Find**.

To find a record:

1 Click the **Find...** button on the Data Form
2 Enter the text you are looking for in the **Find what:** field
3 Select the field it is in from the **In field:** list
4 Click **Find First**
5 If the record displayed isn't the one you want, click **Find Next** until you reach the record required
6 Close the **Find in Field** dialog box when you reach the correct record

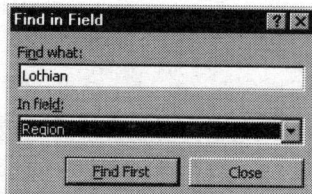

To edit a record:

1 Display the record you want to edit
2 Delete, insert or edit the data in the fields as required

To delete a record:

1 View the record you want to delete
2 Click the **Delete** button

If you edit a record, and then change your mind and want the record as it was originally, you can restore it.

To restore a record:

• Click the **Restore** button

You can also edit the records in your data file in Source view, rather than through the Data Form. Source view displays your data in a table, so you can use any table editing techniques to work on the data – many of the functions are available through the Database toolbar.

If you want to add, remove or rename fields in your data file, do it from Source view.

To manage your fields:

1 Take the data file into Source view

2 Click the **Manage Fields** tool on the Database toolbar

3 Add, remove or rename fields as required

4 Click **OK**

• Remember to SAVE any changes you make to your data source file.

10.5 The main document

Once your data source file is complete, you can create or complete the main document. Either leave the data source file open and move to the Mail Merge Main Document using the Database toolbar or close the data source file (the link between the main document and the data source file will still exist).

To move to the main document from the data source file:

1 If the Data Form is displayed, click the **View Source** button

2 Click the **Mail Merge Main Document** tool on the Database toolbar

To close the data source document:

1 If the Data Form is displayed, click the **View Source** button

2 Click the **Close** button on the title bar of the data source file, or open the **File** menu and choose **Close**

Your main document will contain:

• Standard text for your letter.

• Field names contained in the data source document – so that Word can insert the detail from each record in the correct place in the letter.

• Formatting and layout options as required.

To complete your main document:

1 Modify the page setup, tabs, etc, if necessary

2 Type in any standard text

3 Position the insertion point where you wish to insert data from the data source file

4 Click the **Insert Merge Field** button on the Mail Merge toolbar to display the list of field names from the data source file

5 Select the field name that contains the data from the **Insert Merge Field** list (the contents of the field in the data source file will appear when you produce the result document)

- Merge fields can be included several times in the same main document if necessary – as in the address and salutation of this example.

- Use the spacebar and/or **[Enter]** key to lay out your fields as required.

6 Save the main document

The field names appear within <<chevrons>> in your main document. If field codes appear, e.g. {MERGEFIELD Fieldname} – it is because the option to view the field codes is switched on.

Press **[Alt]-[F9]** to toggle the display of the field codes.

MS/

16 July 1997

«Title» «FirstName» «LastName»
«JobTitle»
«Company»
«Address1»
«Address2»
«Town»
«Region»
«PostalCode»

Dear «Title» «LastName»

INTERNET & INTRANETS – EDINBURGH CONFERENCE CENTRE

—————— 10.6 The result document ——————

Once your main document and data source file have been set up, you can produce your result document.

There are several options to choose from when merging the data from the data file with the main document – try them out to see how they work.

VIEWING THE MERGED DATA

To get a better idea of how the result document will look, you can merge the data of an individual record and view it on screen.

To merge an individual record from the data source file:

1   Click the **View Merged Data** tool 〈〉 – the data from the first data record will be displayed in the main document

2   Use the First Record, Previous Record, Next Record, Last Record buttons on the Mail Merge toolbar to display data from other records if you want to – or enter the record number you want to display in the **Go To Record** box and press **[Enter]**

•   To print the main document with the data currently displayed, click the **Print** tool on the Standard toolbar.

•   Click the **View Merged Data** tool to redisplay the field codes.

MERGING ALL THE RECORDS

You can collect the results into a new document before you print, or you can send the results of the merge directly to your printer.

To collect the result documents into a new document:

1   View the main document in the active window

2   Click the **Merge to New Document** tool 🗐

Each result document is placed in a separate *section* within the new document.

If you want to add information to some of the result documents before you print, use this method and work through your new document editing as required.

- To print the new result document, click the **Print** tool on the Standard toolbar.

To output a result document directly to the printer:

1. View the main document in the active window
2. Click the **Merge to Printer** tool 🖳

10.7 Sorting records

The result document will be easier to use if the records are sorted into ascending or descending alphabetic order on the contact name (rather than the order in which the records were entered).

To sort the data file as it is merged:

1 View the main document
2 Click the Mail Merge tool 🖳
3 Choose **Query Options...**

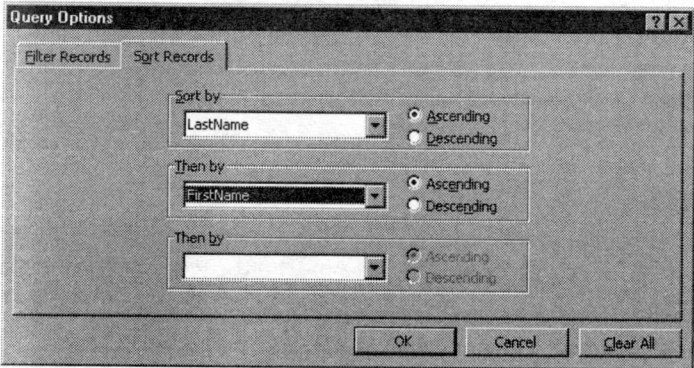

4 Select the **Sort Records** tab
5 Specify the sort fields – you can sort on up to 3 levels
6 Click **OK**
7 Complete the **Merge** dialog box as required – in this case I'd recommend merging to a new document
8 Click **Merge**

This result document lists the records in the order specified.

- If necessary, change the column widths in your result document to ensure that your data looks good.
- If you want a heading at the top of your list, or column headings, add them to your result document.
- Save and print the result document.

To create a list, choose Catalog... at Step 1 in the Merge Helper dialog box. Use tabs or a table to lay out the main document

TELEPHONE LIST		
Contact Name	Company	Telephone No
Paul Allan	Industrial Sciences & Chemicals Ltd	08687 1234
Johanne Andrews	Andrews Design Ltd	0141 445 5544
Jenny Gilmore	New Wave Designs plc	01692 44421
Steven Johnston	Swanson Electrical plc	01606 44312
William Jones	Happy Homes plc	012667 553399
Margaret McPherson	McPherson Foods	01904 555 121
Brenda Simpson	Good Food Ltd	08616 321
Peter Watson	PW Transport plc	01507 445 2211

10.8 Filtering records

If you don't want all the records merged with your main document you can set up selection rules to filter out the records not required.

To filter the data file as it is merged:

1 View the main document in the active window
2 Click the **Mail Merge** tool
3 Choose **Query Options...**
4 Select the **Filter Records** tab
5 Set up your selection rules – to get all the records where the Country is Scotland you would:

- Choose a field from the field list, e.g. *Country*
- Select the required comparison, e.g. *Equal to*
- Type in what it should be compared with, e.g. *Scotland*

6 Click **OK**
7 Complete the **Merge** dialog box as required
8 Click **Merge**

Selection rules

You can specify up to six selection rules. These rules can be connected using AND or OR.

- If all the selection rules listed are to be met before a record is included in the merge, choose AND.
- If you want a record included using different selection rules, choose OR to separate each rule, or set of rules.

If you want to merge all records with 'Scotland' or 'England' in the *Country* field, you need two selection rules connected by OR

If you want to merge all records that contain 'Scotland' in the *Country* field AND 'Perth' in the *Town* field OR 'England' in the *Country* field.

The example below will merge all records where the *Country* field contains 'Scotland' OR 'England' except those records where the *Town* field contains 'York'.

——10.9 Mailing labels and envelopes——

You can produce mailing labels or envelopes for your letters using the mail merge feature. The example here is for mailing labels – if you print onto envelopes, select **Envelopes...** at step 3 below – the dialog boxes that appear are very similar, only with options for envelope sizes rather than labels.

1 Create a new document. This will become your main document
2 Open the **Tools** menu and choose **Mail Merge...**
3 Choose **Create**, then **Mailing Labels** at step 1 in the **Mail Merge Helper** dialog box
4 Select **Active Window** at the prompt
5 Go to step 2, click **Get Data**
6 Locate and select the data source file (the one you created in 10.3 and 10.4 will do)
7 Click **Open**
8 Click **Set Up The Main Document** at the prompt

You are taken into the Label Options dialog box so you can specify the label layout you will be using.

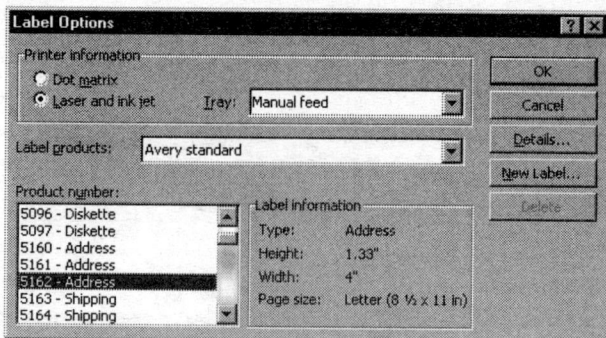

1 Edit the **Printer information** if necessary
2 Choose the **Label products** options required
3 Select the **Product number**
• If you want further information on the label click **Details...**
• If you want to set up a custom label click **New Label...**
4 Click **OK**
• Set up the label in the **Create Labels** dialog box and click **OK**.

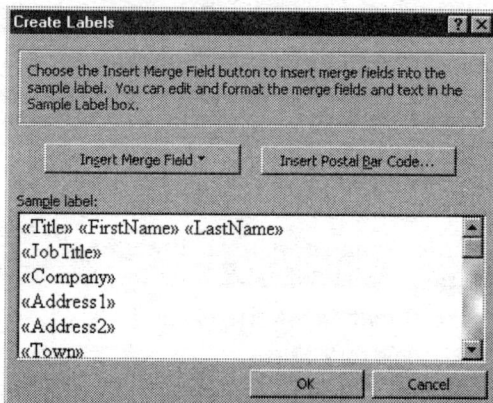

You are returned to the **Mail Merge Helper** dialog box.

Merge to a New Document so that you can check the layout of your labels. If they look okay, save them if you wish, load up your label stationery and print the labels out.

I suggest you save the main document – then you don't need to create the label format again. In future you'll just need to:

1 Open the label format main document file
2 Open the data file that contains the names and addresses (using the **Mail Merge Helper** dialog box)
3 Merge and print out your labels

Dr Paul Allan Development Manager Industrial Sciences & Chemicals Ltd 42 Dunbar Close HADDINGTON Lothian EH30	Miss Johanne Andrews Sales Manager Andrews Design Ltd Hilltop House, 44 Hill Street GLASGOW Strathclyde G14
Mrs Jenny Gilmore Designer New Wave Designs plc 4b Hill Rise LLANARMON Dyffryn-Ceiriog	Mr Steven Johnston Support Technician Swanson Electrical plc 45 High Street WINSFORD Cheshire
Mr William Jones Property Consultant Happy Homes plc 44 York Lane MARTINSTOWN Co Antrim	Mrs Margaret McPherson Director McPherson Foods 231 South View Road YORK Yorkshire
Mrs Brenda Simpson Office Manager Good Food Ltd Orchard House, 24 Orchard Street GIFFORD Lothian EH39	Mr Peter Watson Transport Manager PW Transport plc New Way Industrial Estate, 45 Portlee Road TELFORD Lincs

10.10 Summary

This chapter introduced Mail Merge. We have discussed:

• Setting up different kinds of main document.
• Creating and editing a data source file in Word.
• Creating, editing and updating a main document file.
• Merging the main document and data source file to create a result document.
• Sorting the records to be merged into a specific order.
• Filtering records so that you can include only records that meet the criteria required.
• How to create and print mailing labels and envelopes.

11

PICTURES AND DRAWING

11.1 Aims of this chapter

This chapter discusses some of the ways you can include special text effects, pictures and drawings in your documents. We will consider how you can use WordArt, Clip Art, the Drawing toolbar and picture fonts to add impact to your documents.

11.2 WordArt

You can use WordArt to create eye-catching headings or unusual text effects. You can access WordArt from the Drawing toolbar.

To display the Drawing toolbar:

- Click the **Drawing** tool [icon] on the Standard toolbar.

To insert a WordArt object into your document:

1 Place the insertion point where you want the object to appear
2 Click the **Insert WordArt** tool [icon] on the Drawing toolbar
3 Select a **WordArt style** and click **OK**
4 Enter your text – editing the font as required – and click **OK**

WordArt Gallery

Select a WordArt style:

Edit WordArt Text

Font: Times New Roman   Size: 36   **B** *I*

Text:

Teach Yourself Books

OK   Cancel

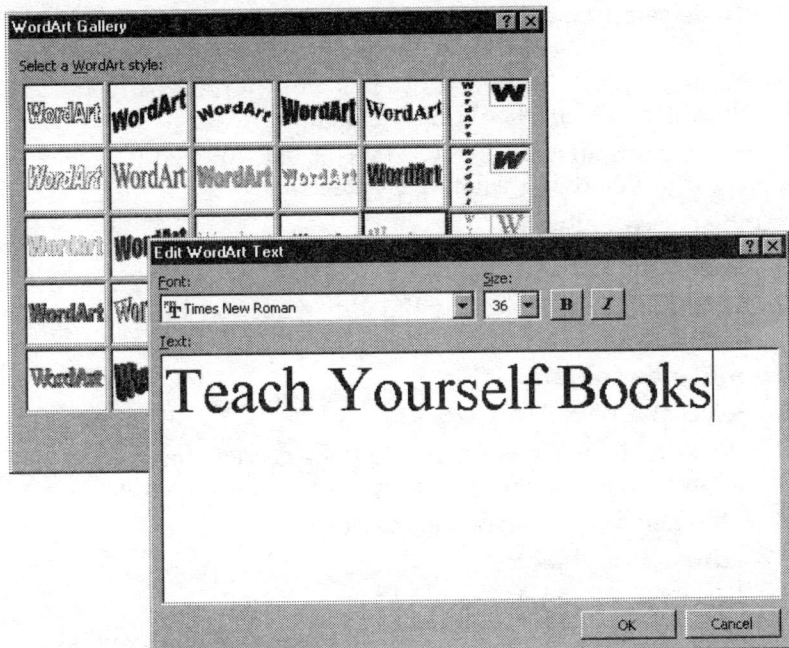

The WordArt object appears in your document. It is currently
selected – it has 'handles' in each corner and along each side,
and an adjust handle (the yellow diamond).

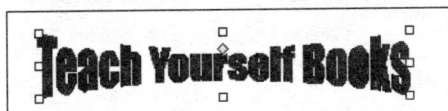

Teach Yourself Books

The WordArt toolbar is displayed.

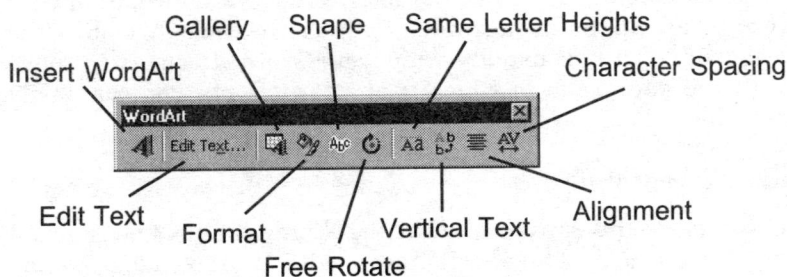

Insert WordArt

Gallery   Shape   Same Letter Heights

Character Spacing

WordArt

Edit Text...

Edit Text   Format   Free Rotate   Vertical Text   Alignment

- To de-select your WordArt object, click anywhere outside it. The WordArt toolbar will disappear when you de-select.
- To select the object again, click anywhere within it. The WordArt toolbar should appear again.

You can manipulate your WordArt object – resize it, move it, adjust it or delete it – when it is selected.

To resize the object:
1 Select the WordArt object
2 Click and drag one of the handles – not the adjust one – in the direction you want to resize it

To move the object:
1 Select the WordArt object
2 Move the mouse pointer inside the selected object – a 4-way arrow symbol appear at the tip of the mouse pointer
3 Drag and drop to move the object

To adjust the object:
1 Select the WordArt object
2 Click and drag the adjust handle to get the effect you want

To delete the object:
1 Select the WordArt object
2 Press the **[Delete]** key on your keyboard

Anchor options

The WordArt object you create is attached to a paragraph. If you display your non-printing characters, you will notice an anchor to the left of the paragraph to which the WordArt object is attached. You will usually want your WordArt object to move with the paragraph to which it is attached, but you can easily override this if you wish.

Move object with text

If you move the paragraph that the WordArt object is attached to, the WordArt object will move with it. If you delete the paragraph that the WordArt object is attached to, the WordArt object will be deleted too. This is because the default settings are to move the object with the text.

If you wish to move the paragraph without moving the WordArt object you must disconnect the two. To do so:

1   Click the **Format WordAr**t tool 🖼️
2   Select the **Position** tab
3   De-select the **Move object with text** checkbox
4   Click **OK**

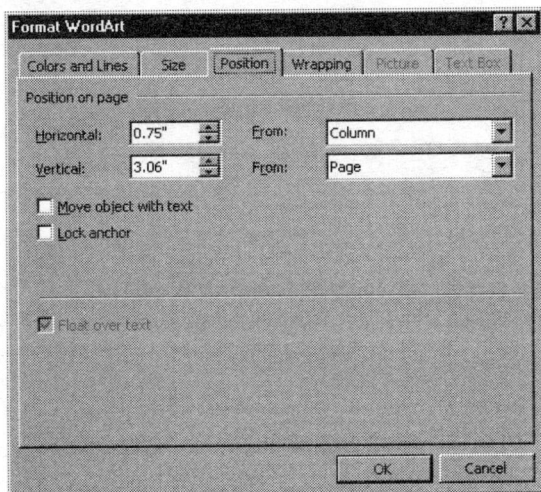

You can now move the paragraph without moving the WordArt object. However, if you delete the paragraph (including the paragraph mark at the end of the paragraph), the WordArt object will also be deleted.

LOCK ANCHOR

If the **Lock anchor** checkbox is selected, the WordArt object will always appear on the same page as the paragraph to which it is attached.

There are several other options for editing and controlling your WordArt object. Experiment with them as you work.

1 Select the WordArt object, then ...
To change the selected style:
2 Click the **WordArt Gallery** tool 🖼
3 Choose another style and click **OK**
To edit the text in the WordArt object:
2 Click the **Edit Text...** tool
3 Modify the text as required and click **OK**
To change the format of your WordArt object:
2 Click the **Format WordArt** tool 🖌
3 Experiment with the options in the dialog box
To change the WordArt shape:
2 Click the **WordArt Shape** tool 🔤
3 Select from the shapes displayed
To rotate the WordArt object:
2 Click the **Free Rotate** tool 🔄
3 Drag a rotate handle (a green circle) to rotate the object
4 Click the **Free Rotate** tool again
To make upper and lower case characters the same height:
2 Click the **WordArt Same Letter Heights** tool 🔠
3 If you change your mind, click again to cancel the effect
Try out the other tools. You can:
• Display your text vertically rather then horizontally.
• Change the alignment of your text.
• Alter the spacing between your characters.

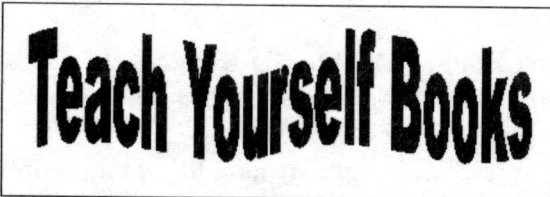

Teach Yourself Books

11.3 Clip Art

If you've installed Microsoft Office you'll find you've access to lots of Clip Art – if you've bought the CD version of Office, you've even more to choose from than with the diskette version.

To insert Clip Art:

1 Choose **Picture** from the **Insert** menu

2 Select **Clip Art**

3 Insert the Office CD if you want access to all the clip art that's available (if the Office or Office Pro folder opens, close it)

4 Click **OK**

• The **Microsoft Clip Gallery 3.0** dialog box opens, with the **Clip Art** tab selected.

5 Select a Clip Art category

6 Scroll through the clips and select one you want to use

7 Click **Insert**

The clip you have inserted can be resized, moved or deleted using the same techniques as for a WordArt object (see 11.2 above).

To replace your clip with a different image, double click on the clip to open the clip art dialog box again, and choose a new clip.

If you find scrolling through the clips a bit tedious, you can always use the **Find...** options to locate Clip Art that may be suitable.

1 Choose **Picture** from the **Insert** menu

2 Select **Clip Art**

3 Click the **Find...** button

4 Enter the keyword you're looking for, e.g. *tree* in the **Keywords** field

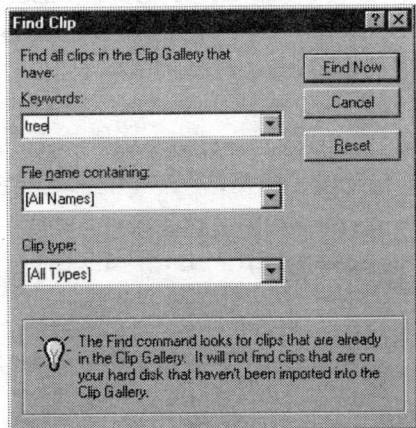

5 Click **Find Now**

6   If your keyword is recognised, a list of clips that match your
    keyword will be displayed

The clips that you insert into your document can be formatted in
a number of ways – the best thing to do is experiment with the
options and see what effect they have.

When a clip is selected the Picture toolbar is displayed. You can
use the toolbar to modify your picture.

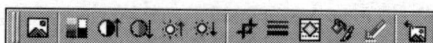

Working from left to right on the toolbar:

- **Insert Picture** – inserts a picture from File rather than from
  the Microsoft Gallery.

- **Image Control** – *Automatic* is the default.

  Greyscale converts each colour to a different shade of grey.

  Black and white converts the picture to a black and white
  picture.

  Watermark converts the object to a low contrast picture that
  you can place behind everything else to create a watermark.

- **More Contrast** – increase the contrast.

- **Less Contrast** – decrease the contrast.

- **Increase Brightness** – increase the brightness.

- **Decrease Brightness** – decrease the brightness.

- **Crop** – lets you trim the edges of the clip.

  To crop a clip:

  1   Select it

  2   Click the **Crop** tool

3   Drag a resizing handle to cut off the bits you don't want

- **Line Style** – puts lines around the picture.

- **Text wrap** – allows you to specify how you want your text to
  wrap around your picture.

- **Format Picture** – opens the Format Picture dialog box where
  you have access to even more formatting options.

- **Set Transparent Color** – only available with drawing objects (those created using the drawing tools on the Drawing toolbar – see 11.4 below).
- **Reset Picture** – returns the clip to its original state

Explore the other tabs in the Microsoft Gallery. You'll find pictures, sounds and videos that you can use.

If you insert a sound or video into your document, double click on the object to replay it.

11.4 Drawing

You can use the Drawing toolbar to add different effects to your document and also to draw your own pictures. You should be in Page Layout view when drawing.

Line, Arrow, Rectangle and Oval

The basic tools are the Line, Arrow, Rectangle and Oval. You can use these tools to draw basic lines and shapes.

To use these tools:
1 Click the tool
2 Click and drag to draw the shape

To get a perfect square or circle, select the Rectangle or Oval tool, and then hold the **[Shift]** key down as you click and drag.

To resize or move your drawing objects:
1 Select the object – click on it
- Click and drag a handle to resize the object.
- Click and drag within the object to move it.
2 De-select the object

To delete a drawing object:

1 Select the object
2 Press the **[Delete]** key on your keyboard

To add a shadow or 3-D effect to your object:

1 Select the object
2 Click the **Shadow** tool ▣ or **3-D** tool ▣ on the Drawing toolbar
3 Choose the effect you want
4 De-select the object

To change a line or arrow style of an object:

1 Select the object you want to change
2 Click the **Line Style** ≡, **Dash Style** ▤ or **Arrow Style** ⇄ tool
3 Choose the effect you want
4 De-select the object

To change the fill colour or line colour of an object:

1 Select the object
2 Click the drop down arrow to the right of the **Fill** ▨▾ or **Line Color** ✎▾ tool
3 Choose a colour
4 De-select the object

Text Boxes

You can add text anywhere in your document if it is contained within a Text Box.

To insert a Text Box:

1 Click the Text Box tool
2 Click and drag within your document to create your Text Box
3 Type in the text you want to appear in the Text Box
4 De-select the object

When a Text Box is selected, the Text Box toolbar is displayed.

Create Link ——
Text Box ✕
——Change Text Direction

Break Link   Previous   Next

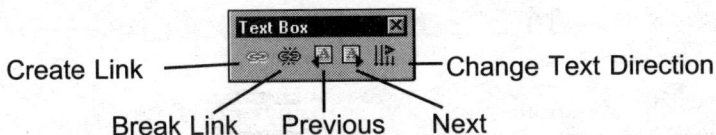

You can use this toolbar to link Text Boxes so that the overspill from one Text Box flows into the next one. You can also use it to change the alignment of text within your Text Boxes.

To link Text Boxes:

| The text in this Text Box | flows to the Text Box it is linked to |

1 Create a Text Box and enter your text into it
2 Create another Text Box, but leave it empty
3 Select the first Text Box
4 Click the **Create Link** tool on the Text Box toolbar
5 Click on the empty Text Box that you want to link to

As you enter text in the first Text Box, it will flow automatically to the linked Text Box when the first box is full.

The other tools are used to break the link between Text Boxes, to move between linked Text Boxes and to change text direction.

AutoShapes

If you want to draw stars, banners, block arrows, flow chart symbols, etc, you may find the shape you need in the AutoShapes.

1 Click the **AutoShapes** tool on the Drawing toolbar
2 Choose a category
3 Select a shape
4 Click and drag to draw your shape

AutoShapes in action

This is a Callout – it is used just like a Text Box – see above

——— 11.5 Some more options ———

The Draw tool on the Drawing toolbar gives access to yet more options. Some of them are introduced here.

To open the Draw menu, click on the drop-down arrow to the right of the Draw tool on the Drawing toolbar.

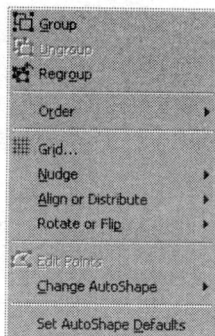

Group
Ungroup
Regroup
Order ▶
Grid...
Nudge ▶
Align or Distribute ▶
Rotate or Flip ▶
Edit Points
Change AutoShape ▶
Set AutoShape Defaults

Grouping

If you are drawing a picture using different drawing objects, you will find your final picture easier to resize and move if you Group the objects together.

Before you can group several objects, you must select them.

To select more than one object at a time:

1 Select the first object required – click on it
2 Hold the **[Shift]** key down while you click on each of the other objects

or

1 Click the **Select Objects** tool on the Drawing toolbar
2 Click and drag over the objects you want

To group objects:

1 Select the objects you want to group
2 Open the **Draw** menu
3 Choose **Group**

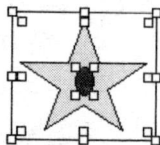

The objects are grouped together into one object and can then be resized, moved or deleted as one.

If you need to work on an individual object that has been grouped, you can ungroup the object again.

To ungroup an object:

1 Select the object you want to ungroup

2 Open the **Draw** menu

3 Choose **Ungroup**

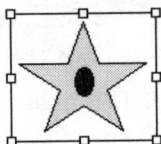

Objects than have been ungrouped, can quickly be regrouped:

1 Open the **Draw** menu

2 Choose **Regroup**

Order

When you draw your objects on top of each other, the first one you draw is on the lowest layer, the second one is on a layer above the first one, the third one on the next layer and so on. If you end up with your objects on the wrong layer relative to each other, you can move them backwards and forwards through the layers as necessary.

To move an object from one layer to another, relative to other objects:

1 Select the object

2 Choose **Order** from the Draw menu

3 Move the object as required

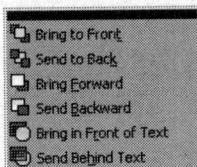

- **Bring to Front** and **Send to Back** move the object to the top or bottom layer respectively.

- **Bring Forward** and **Send Backward** move the object one layer at a time.

- **Bring in Front of Text** and **Send Behind Text** places the selected drawing object in front of or behind text. The default option is that a drawing object is placed in front of text.

Rotate or Flip

Objects can also be rotated by any amount, or flipped 180 degrees horizontally or vertically.

To rotate an object:

1 Select the object

2 Click the **Free Rotate** tool 🔄 on the drawing toolbar

3 Click and drag the rotate handles (small green circles) until the object is in the position required

4 Select another tool, or click the **Free Rotate** tool again, when you've finished

To flip an object:

1 Select the object

2 Choose **Rotate or Flip** from the Draw drop-down list

3 Select a rotate or flip option

11.6 Picture fonts

You can also use any picture fonts that you have installed on your system to give you pictures.

To access the picture fonts:

1 Open the **Insert** menu and choose **Symbol**

2 Explore the fonts until you find a picture you want to use

3 Select the picture

4 Click **Insert**

5 Close the **Symbol** dialog box

You can format the character you have inserted using the Formatting toolbar or the Font dialog box – you can make it bold or put it into italics, change its size or colour, etc.

Explore the fonts that you have available to you to see if they contain any pictures that you would find useful.

11.7 Summary

In this chapter we have discussed some of the options available when you want to include special effects and pictures in a document. The main options are:

- WordArt
- Clip Art
- Drawing
- Picture Fonts

12

MACROS

12.1 Aims of this chapter

We have already discussed some of the features that help you automate the way you work in Word. In this chapter we will consider how macros can help you automate your work. Macros are useful when you want to automate a routine that you perform regularly. In this chapter we will discuss some areas in which you may find macros useful. You will learn how to record, play back and edit the macros you create.

12.2 What are macros?

A macro is a set of Word commands grouped together so that you can execute them as a single command.

If you perform a task often, but cannot find a Word keyboard shortcut, or tool, that runs through the sequence you want to use, you should *record* the commands into a macro. You have then created a 'custom' command.

What could you use a macro for?

- Speeding up routine editing and formatting.
- Recording the instructions to create a new document using one of your own templates – your letterhead, memo or fax.
- Quickly accessing an option you regularly use in a dialog box.
- Combining a group of commands you often execute in the same sequence.

There are two ways to create macros in Word:

1 **Macro Recorder** We will be using this option. You can use the Macro Recorder to record any function that you can access through the menus and dialog boxes.

2 **Visual Basic Editor** You can record powerful, flexible macros using the Visual Basic Editor. These macros can include Visual Basic commands as well as Word commands. We will take a brief excursion into the Visual Basic Editor when we discuss editing macros.

———— 12.3 Recording your macro ————

Before you start recording your macro, think through what it is that you want to record. If there are any commands that you're not sure about, try them out first to check that they do what you want to record.

Try recording a simple macro that prints the current page.

To print the current page, you must:

1 Choose **Print** from the **File** menu
2 Select **Current page** in the **Page Range** options
3 Click **OK**

Once you know what you need to record, you can create your macro.

In the example below we will assign the macro to a tool on a toolbar and also assign it a keyboard shortcut.

To start recording a macro:

1 Open the **Tools** menu and choose **Macro**

2 Select **Record New Macro...**

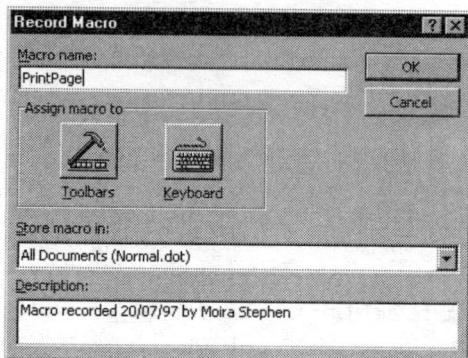

3 Enter a name for your macro in the **Macro name** field (don't use the default Macro1, Macro2, etc – you'll never remember what you record in each one)

To assign your macro to a toolbar (optional):

1 Click **Toolbars** in the **Record Macro** dialog box

2 The **Customize** dialog box appears

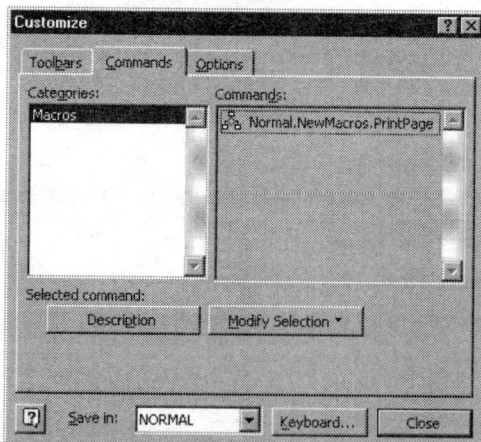

3 Drag the macro name from the **Commands:** list and drop it onto a toolbar that is currently displayed on screen

To change the button image:

1 With the tool on the toolbar still selected, click **Modify Selection** in the **Customize** dialog box

2 To display the button only, choose the **Default Style** (if you opt to display text with the button, each tool takes up a lot of space)

3 Click **Modify Selection** again

4 Select **Change Button Image**

5 Choose a button for your toolbar

6 Click **Close**

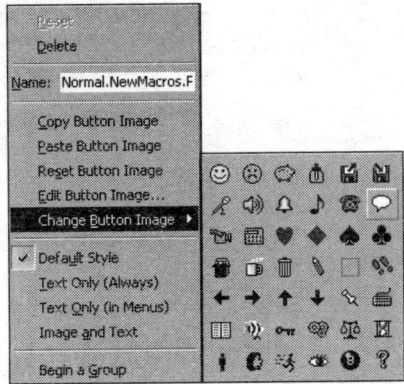

To assign a keyboard shortcut to your macro (optional):

1 Click **Keyboard** at the **Record Macro** or **Customize** dialog box

2 Enter a keyboard shortcut in the **Press new shortcut key:** field (you'll be prompted if the shortcut is already in use)

3 Click **Assign** and close the **Customize Keyboard** dialog box

4 Close the **Customize** dialog box if necessary

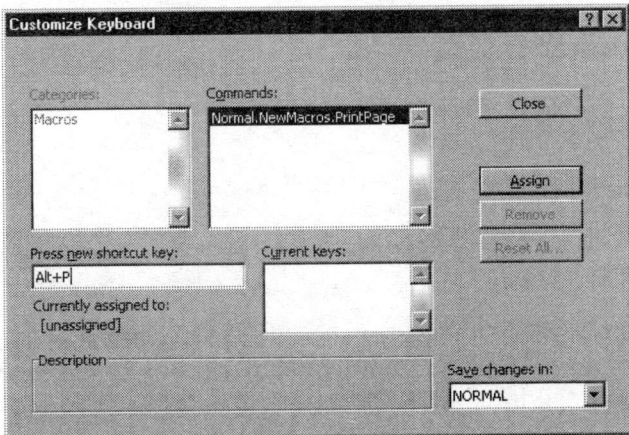

You will be returned to your document, and the **Stop Recording** toolbar will be displayed.

To record your macro:

1 Perform the sequence of commands you want to record (if you are recording the steps to print the current page, click **OK** at the print dialog box to send the page to the printer)

• If you need to temporarily stop recording your macro (perhaps to check something out) click the **Pause Recording** tool. The tool then becomes the **Resume Recorder** tool – click it when you're ready to start recording again.

2 Click the **Stop Recording** tool when you've finished

——— 12.4 Playing back your macro ———

If you assigned your macro to a toolbar:

• Click the tool on the toolbar to run the macro.

If you gave your macro a keyboard shortcut

• Press the keyboard shortcut keys to run the macro.

An alternative to running the macro from the keyboard or toolbar is to replay it through the **Tools** menu.

1 Open the **Tools** menu and select **Macro**
2 Choose **Macros...**
3 Select the macro you want to replay from the list
4 Click **Run**

——— 12.5 Ideas for more macros ———

You can record almost anything you want into a macro. Some of the things that you could record into a macro may also be automated in other ways, e.g. AutoText or Styles.

Macros are usually used to carry out a sequence of commands, or to perform tasks you would normally need to dig into a dialog box to find.

Try out the macros below to get some more practice. They are all easy to set up. You can assign the macros to keyboard shortcuts or to tools on a toolbar if you wish.

- Record three separate macros. Each will create a new document, one using your letter template, one using your memo template and one using your fax template (you could call the macros *Letter*, *Memo* and *Fax* respectively).

You would need to record the steps:

1 Open the **File** menu
2 Choose **New**
3 Select the template you want to base your new document on
4 Click **OK**

- Record a macro to send the current document to print, close it and create a new blank document (you could call the macro *PrintCloseNew*).

You would need to record the steps:

1 Print the file
2 Close the file
3 Create a new blank document

A FORMATTING MACRO

If you regularly apply the same formatting to a table row, record the formatting in a macro. (You could call the macro *FormatRow*)

Place the insertion point at the beginning of a row before you start to record.

For example, to format a row to have shading of 30%, font Arial, font size 16, font colour red, with the cell contents centred, you would need to record:

1 Select the entire row, by pressing **[Shift]-[Alt]-[End]** (you must use keyboard shortcuts to select when recording macros)

2 Open the **Format** menu and choose **Borders and Shading...**
3 Select the **Shading** tab and set the shading to 30%
4 Use the Formatting toolbar to set the font formatting options

──────────12.6 Deleting a macro──────────

As you experiment with setting up macros, you will inevitably end up with some that you don't want to keep. They may not prove as useful as you first thought, or they may not run properly.

To delete a macro that you no longer require:

1 Open the **Tools** menu and select **Macro**
2 Choose **Macros...**
3 Select the Macro you want to delete from the list displayed
4 Click **Delete**
5 Confirm the deletion at the prompt
6 Click **Close**

If necessary, remove the tool that executed the macro from the toolbar it was on – see 13.4 in the next chapter.

──────────12.7 Editing a macro──────────

I'd suggest you re-record any short macro that has an error in it rather than try to edit it – if it's a short macro you can probably re-record it as quickly as you could edit it.

However, if you have recorded a longer macro or have a minor adjustment to make to a macro, it's probably quicker to edit it rather than re-record the whole thing again.

The macros you record through the Macro Recorder are translated into Visual Basic – so things may look a bit strange when you first try editing a macro. But don't worry, if you take your time and have a look through the instructions you'll soon be able to relate your actions in Word to the Visual Basic code.

When editing a macro, be very careful not to delete anything you don't understand, or insert anything that should not be there – you might find your macro no longer runs properly if you do.

If the worst comes to the worst and the macro stops working, you can always record it again.

In this example, I'm going to edit the *FormatRow* macro (see section 12.5 above) to have a font size of 18 rather than 16.

To edit the macro:

1 Open the **Tools** menu and select **Macro**
2 Choose **Macros...**
3 Select the macro you want to edit from the list and click **Edit**
4 Scroll through the code until you see the line you want to edit

```
NORMAL - NewMacros [Code]
(General)                          FormatRow

            End With
            With .Borders(wdBorderVertical)
                .LineStyle = wdLineStyleSingle
                .LineWidth = wdLineWidth050pt
                .ColorIndex = wdAuto
            End With
            .Borders.Shadow = False
        End With
        With Options
            .DefaultBorderLineStyle = wdLineStyleSingle
            .DefaultBorderLineWidth = wdLineWidth050pt
            .DefaultBorderColorIndex = wdAuto
        End With
        Selection.Font.Name = "Arial"
        Selection.Font.Size = 16
        Selection.Font.ColorIndex = wdRed
        Selection.ParagraphFormat.Alignment = wdAlignParagraph
```

5 Edit as required – I deleted the *16* and typed in *18* at *Selection.Font.Size*
6 Click the **Save Normal** tool on the toolbar
7 Close the Visual Basic Editor – click the **Close** button or choose **Close and Return to Microsoft Word** from the **File** menu

When you look through the Visual Basic code there are often far more lines of code than commands you intentionally recorded through the Macro Recorder. Don't worry about this – some instructions are picked up from default settings in dialog boxes. Just scroll through until you see something you recognise as the line you want to change.

12.8 Summary

In this chapter we have discussed macros. You have learnt how to:

• Record a macro using the Macro Recorder.
• Assign the macro to a toolbar.
• Give the macro a keyboard shortcut.
• Play back, or run, the macro.
• Delete a macro.
• Edit a macro using the Visual Basic Editor.

13

TOOLBARS

13.1 Aims of this chapter

In this chapter we discuss toolbars. We'll look at basic toolbar manipulation – the positioning of toolbars on the screen and showing and hiding toolbars. We'll also discuss how you can edit existing toolbars, create new toolbars and assign macros to toolbars (ones that you didn't assign when you set the macro up).

13.2 Moving toolbars

When working in Word the Standard toolbar and Formatting toolbar are normally displayed along the top of your screen – the Standard one above the Formatting one.

Toolbars can be positioned anywhere on your screen. There are four docking areas – at the top, bottom, left and right of your screen, and your toolbars can be placed in any of them. You can also leave your toolbar floating in the document area if you prefer.

To move a toolbar:

If the toolbar is docked

1   Point to the left edge of the toolbar (if the toolbar is docked at the top or bottom of the screen) or top edge (if the toolbar is docked at the left or right of the screen) – where the two raised lines are

2   Drag and drop the toolbar to the position you want it in

If the toolbar is not docked

1   Point to its Title Bar

2   Drag and drop the toolbar to the position you want it in

—— 13.3 Showing and hiding toolbars ——

You will have noticed that some toolbars appear and disappear automatically when you are working in Word. You can also opt to show or hide toolbars whenever you want to use the tools on them.

Provided you have at least one toolbar displayed, you can use the shortcut method to show or hide any toolbar.

To use the shortcut method:

1   Point to a toolbar

2   Click the right mouse button

•   Any toolbars that are displayed have a tick beside their name, any that are not displayed have no tick.

3   Click (using the left mouse button) on the toolbar name you wish to show or hide

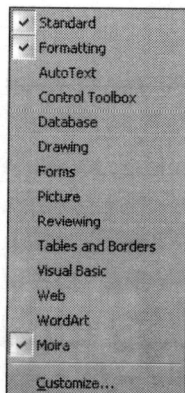

If no toolbars are displayed, you must use the View menu to show them again.

1   Open the **View** menu and choose **Toolbars**

2   Click on the one you want to show

Using either of the methods above, you can show or hide one toolbar at a time. If you want to change the display status of several toolbars at the one time, it may be quicker to use the Customize dialog box.

1 Right click on a toolbar that is currently displayed

or

Open the **View** menu and choose **Toolbars**

2 Click **Customize...**

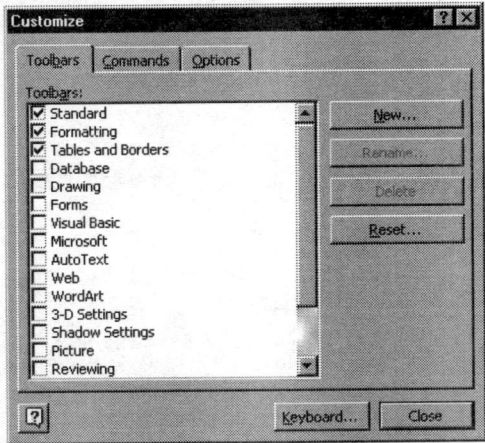

3 Select or deselect the toolbars in the list as required (a tick means they are displayed, no tick means they are hidden)

4 Click **Close**

——— 13.4 Editing existing toolbars ———

If you find that there are some tools on a toolbar that you never tend to use, or if you want to add another tool to a toolbar, you can edit the toolbar. If you want to add several tools to a toolbar, you should create a new toolbar and add your tools to it – see 13.5 below. If you want to edit a toolbar it must be displayed.

To edit an existing toolbar:

1 Display the toolbar you want to edit if necessary
2 Right click on a toolbar that is currently displayed

or

Open the **View** menu and choose **Toolbars**
3 Click **Customize...**
4 Select the **Commands** tab

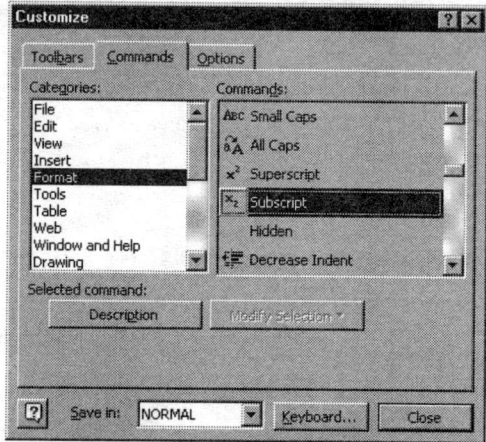

To add a tool:

1 Select the **Category** of tool you're looking for
2 Locate the tool you require in the list
3 Drag it over to the toolbar – when you are over a toolbar a very dark I-beam with a **+** beside it indicates your position. Drop it in the position required (if you are not over a toolbar, the mouse pointer has a small button with an **x**)

If you want a brief description of a tool's purpose, select it in the list of commands on the **Commands** tab, or on the toolbar, then click the **Description** button.

To move a tool:

1 Drag the tool to the correct position on the toolbar
2 Drop it

To remove a tool:

1 Drag the tool off the toolbar
2 Drop it anywhere
• Click **Close** when you've finished editing your toolbar.

The drop-down lists that appear on toolbars, e.g. Style box and Font box on the Formatting toolbar take up a lot more room than one of the picture tools.

If you need to make more space on a toolbar that contains drop-down tools, you can change the size of these tools as required.

To change the size of a drop-down tool, you must have the **Customize** dialog box open.

1 Select the tool you want to resize e.g. [Normal ▼]
2 Click and drag the right or left edge of it – the mouse pointer becomes a thick double-headed arrow when you are in the correct place

---

SHORTCUT

You can quickly move or delete tools from a toolbar that is displayed without opening the Customize dialog box.

To move a tool: Hold down the **[Alt]** key and drag the tool along the toolbar (or to another toolbar)

To delete a tool: Hold down the **[Alt]** key and drag the tool off the toolbar

---

——— 13.5 Creating a new toolbar ———

If you have several tools that you'd like to add to a toolbar (or macros that you want to assign to tools), you may find that you need to create a new toolbar, rather than try to squeeze tools into the existing toolbars.

To create a new toolbar:

1 Right click on a toolbar that is currently displayed

or

Open the **View** menu and choose **Toolbars**

2 Click **Customize...**

3 Select the **Toolbars** tab

4 Click **New...**

5 Give your toolbar a name and click **OK**

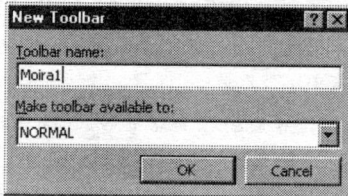

6 Your toolbar will be displayed

7 Choose the **Commands** tab and add the tools you require to your new toolbar

8 **Close** the **Customize** dialog box

—13.6 Adding your macros to toolbars—

In the previous chapter we discussed macros – custom commands that you can set up. When setting up your macro, you have the option to assign the macro to a tool on a toolbar. However, if you opt not to add the macro to a toolbar when you create the macro, you can easily assign your macro to a tool at any time.

To assign a macro to a toolbar:

1 Display the toolbar you want to assign your macro to if necessary

2 Right click on a toolbar that is currently displayed

or

Open the **View** menu and choose **Toolbars**

3 Click **Customize...**

4 Choose the **Commands** tab

5 Select the **Macros** category

6 Drag the macro that you want to assign to a tool over to your toolbar

13.7 Summary

In this chapter we have discussed the various options available when working with and modifying toolbars. We have discussed:

- Positioning toolbars on your screen.
- Showing and hiding toolbars.
- Adding tools to toolbars.
- Moving tools on toolbars.
- Removing tools from toolbars.
- Creating new toolbars.
- Assigning macros to a tool.

14

WORD WITH OTHER APPLICATIONS

—————— 14.1 Aims of this chapter ——————

Word is part of the Microsoft Office suite, and it integrates very well with the other applications in the suite. If you have installed the complete Office suite then you have the benefit of being able to use the best tool for the job. This chapter discusses some of the ways in which the Office applications can be integrated.

—————— 14.2 Linking vs embedding ——————

When you work through this chapter, you will come across the terms 'linking' and 'embedding'. Both these techniques enable you to incorporate data from other applications into your Word document.

The main differences between linked and embedded data lie in:

- Where it is stored.
- How it is updated.

Linked data

Linked data is not stored in your Word document. It is stored in a file – e.g. a workbook or presentation – in the source application (the application that it was created in). The data is updated within the source application – and those changes are reflected in the Word document to which it is linked.

Features of linking data include:

• The Word document is kept smaller than it otherwise would have been.

• The data in the Word document reflects the current status of the source data.

Embedded data

Embedded data is stored in your Word document. However, when you create and edit the data, you have access to all the functions within the source application.

Features of embedding data include:

• All the data is held in one document.

• You have access to powerful functions that are not part of the Word application when creating and editing the object.

The following sections discuss some of the methods you can use to integrate the data across the applications in Office.

• Section 14.3 discusses simple copy and paste techniques to get data from one application to another.

• Section 14.4 discusses Paste Special (this option enables you to link the data in one application to another).

• The other sections discuss techniques that are specific to particular packages.

——————14.3 Copy and Paste——————

You can copy text, data, graphics, charts, etc. from one application to another within the Office suite using simple copy and paste techniques.

To copy and paste:
1 Launch Word and the application you want to copy from
2 Select the object, text or data you want to copy
3 Click the **Copy** tool on the Standard toolbar
4 Switch to Word
5 Place the insertion point where you want the object, text or data to appear
6 Click the **Paste** tool on the Standard toolbar

Data pasted in to a Word document from Excel or Access is displayed in a Word table, and can be edited and manipulated using the table-handling features in Word.

When you copy data using this method, it is not linked to the original data in Excel, Access or PowerPoint in any way. Should you edit the data in the source application, the data you copied into Word remains as it was when you copied it.

——————14.4 Copy and Paste Special——————

If you want the data that you copy into your Word document to be kept in line with the data held in the source application, you should create a link to it. You must use Copy and Paste Special to create a link.

You can use paste special to link to files in Excel or PowerPoint.

To create a link to data or a chart in Excel:
1 Open the workbook that contains the data or chart you want to create a link to

WORD WITH OTHER APPLICATIONS

2 Select the data or chart required

3 Click the **Copy** tool

4 Switch to Word

5 Open the document you want to paste into

6 Position the insertion point where you want the data or chart to appear

7 Open the **Edit** menu and choose **Paste Special...**

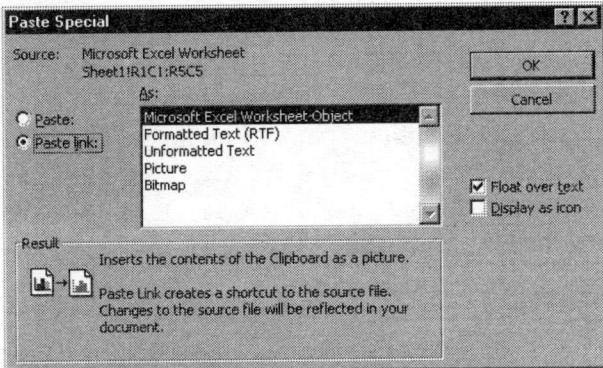

8 Select the **Paste Link** button

9 Choose an option from the **As:** list – when you select an option a brief description of how it works appears in the **Result** box

10 Click **OK**

Sales figures - 1st quarter							
	January		February		March		Total
Brian	£	17,500	£	20,500	£	17,600	£	55,600
Angela	£	15,600	£	14,320	£	13,959	£	43,879
Jack	£	14,760	£	19,500	£	18,300	£	52,560

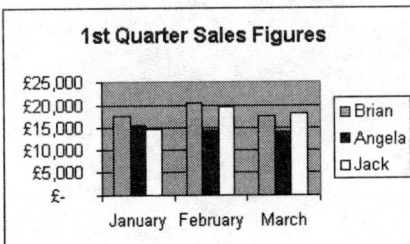

1st Quarter Sales Figures

LINKED OBJECTS

By default, linked objects are set for automatic updating. This means that the destination file in Word is updated automatically each time you open it, or each time the source data in Excel is updated, when the destination file in Word is open. You can change the updating options in Word if you prefer. See *Control how linked objects* are updated in the on-line Help for details of the options available.

To create a link to a slide in PowerPoint:

1 Open the presentation that contains the data you want to create a link to

2 Go into **Slide Sorter** view

3 Select the slide required

4 Click the **Copy** tool

5 Switch to Word

6 Open the document you want to paste into

7 Position the insertion point where you want the slide to appear

8 Open the **Edit** menu and choose **Paste Special...**

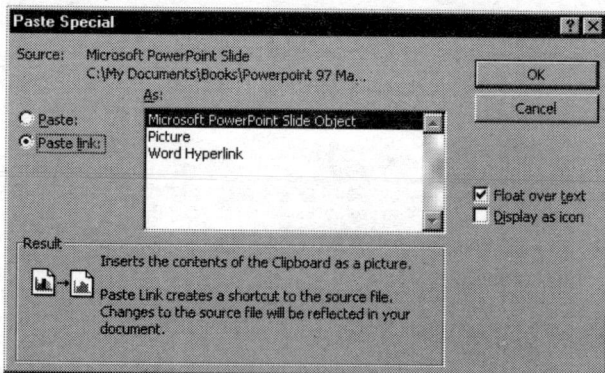

9 Select the **Paste Link** button

10 Choose an option from the **As:** list

11 Click **OK**

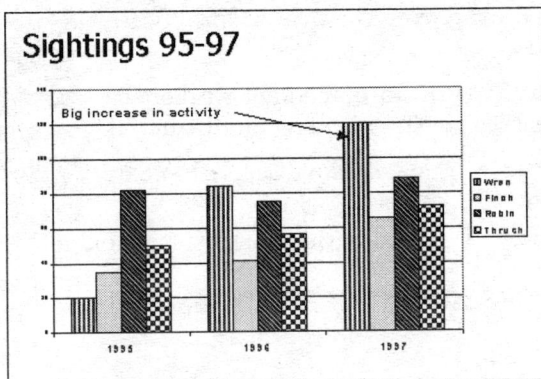

If the PowerPoint presentation is updated, you must save the changes before they will be reflected in your Word document.

The data you insert into your Word document in this way is linked. With linked data, the data is not held in your Word document. It is useful to link data when you need to have the data in Word kept in line with the way things actually are in the source file – whenever the Excel workbook or PowerPoint presentation is updated, the changes will be reflected in your Word document.

————— 14.5 Word and Excel —————

If you want an Excel worksheet in your Word document, but don't need the worksheet for any other purpose, you can insert a worksheet into your document. The worksheet you insert will be created and edited using Excel functions.

The Excel Worksheet you insert will be an 'embedded' object.

To insert a Microsoft Excel Worksheet:

1 Place the insertion point where you want the worksheet to appear
2 Click the **Insert Microsoft Excel Worksheet** tool

3 Click and drag over the grid to specify the worksheet size

• You end up with an embedded worksheet, with the Excel toolbars and menus displayed.

4 Set up your worksheet using Excel's toolbars and menus

5 Click anywhere outside the worksheet when you've finished

	A	B	C	D
1	Clearance Sale			
2		Original Price	Sale Price	
3	Black Bookcase	£ 137.00	£ 68.50	
4				

Sheet 1

• To edit your worksheet, double click on it – you will be returned to Excel.

—— 14.6 Word and PowerPoint ——

In addition to copy and paste or paste special techniques, there are other ways of working between Word and PowerPoint.

PowerPoint presentations from Word documents

You can quickly set up a PowerPoint presentation from a Word document. The Word document must be set up as an outline (see Chapter 8). It is important that you format the text in your Word document using the heading styles 1 – 9 as PowerPoint uses the heading levels to structure the slides it creates.

Text formatted using the Heading 1 style in your Word document will be used for the slide title on each new slide, Heading 2 styles will be used as the first level of bullet points, etc.

To create the presentation:

1 Open your Word document if necessary

2 Choose **Send To** from the **File** menu

3 Click **Microsoft PowerPoint**

Word documents from PowerPoint presentations

You can also quickly generate a Word document from a PowerPoint presentation. The print quality of the presentation is improved if you switch to a black and white colour scheme before you send your presentation (Open the View menu in PowerPoint and click Black and White).

1 Open the presentation you want to create a document from

2 Choose **Send To** from the **File** menu

3 Select **Microsoft Word**

4 Choose a page layout for your document in the **Write-Up** dialog box

5 Select **Paste** or **Paste Link**

6 Click **OK**

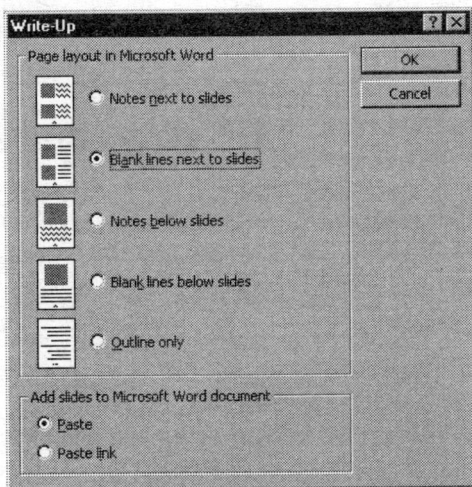

A new document will be created in Word. You can save and/or print the document as required.

If you opt to Paste link, your Word document will automatically update when the PowerPoint presentation is edited and saved.

Meeting Minder

If you use Meeting Minder to take notes as you give a presentation in PowerPoint, you can export the notes and actions to Word at the end of your presentation.

1 Click **Export...** in the **Meeting Minder** dialog box
2 Select **Send meeting minutes and action items to Microsoft Word**
3 Click **Export Now**

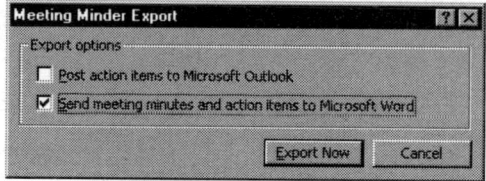

The result is a quickly produced, useful summary of the meeting.

14.7 Word and Access

You can copy and paste from Access in the same way as you did with Excel. You can also use an Access table or query as a data source in a Mail Merge (see Chapter 10).

To use an Access table or query as a Mail Merge data source:

1 Open the tools menu and choose Mail Merge
2 Create your main document
3 At step 2, click **Get data**, then select **Open Data Source**
4 Locate the database that you want to link to your main document
5 Open the database
6 Select the table or query you want to link to
7 Click **OK**

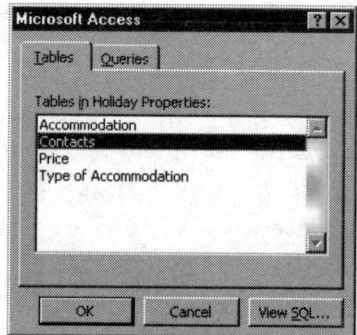

8 Continue through the **Mail Merge** dialog as usual (see Chapter 10)

- You can also link to an Excel worksheet in the same way. If you don't want to link to the entire sheet, make sure you know the named range or cell range you require before you start.

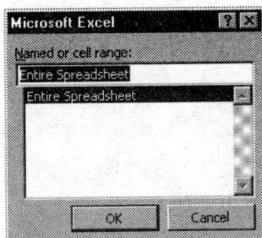

————————— 14.8 Summary ———————————

In this chapter we have discussed some of the ways you can integrate Word with the rest of the Microsoft Office suite. We have discussed:

- Liking and embedding
- Copy and Paste.
- Copy and Paste Special from Excel and PowerPoint.
- Embedding an Excel worksheet.
- Creating a PowerPoint presentation from a Word document.
- Creating a Word document from a PowerPoint presentation.
- Creating minutes in Word from Meeting Minder in PowerPoint.
- Using an Access table or query as the data source document in a Word mail merge.

15

WORD AND THE WEB

15.1 Aims of this chapter

This chapter discusses using Word with the wider world. You will learn how to e-mail a Word document. You will also learn how to use Hyperlinks to link to other files on your own computer or network, and to pages on the World Wide Web. Finally, we'll create a Web document from within Word and discuss how you should go about publishing it to the Web. The examples in this chapter are based on the use of Microsoft Outlook for e-mail. You must also have access to the Internet for this chapter.

15.2 E-mail

Provided you have a modem, communications software and a service provider, you can e-mail your Word documents to anywhere in the world. When you e-mail a document, you send it electronically over a computer network. E-mail is usually very fast – sometimes your message will be delivered almost instantly, other times it may take longer.

As a Word user, you should specify Word as your e-mail editor in Outlook. You can then format your text, create tables, bulleted lists etc using familiar Word features.

To specify Word as your e-mail editor:

1 Start Outlook – click the **Start** button on the Taskbar, choose **Programs** then select **Microsoft Outlook**

2 Open the **Tools** menu and choose **Options...**

3 Select **Use Microsoft Word as the e-mail editor**

4 Click **OK**

Another useful option to have set up in Outlook is the automatic saving of messages that you send.

To check the status of this option on your machine:

1 Open the **Tools** menu in **Outlook**

2 Choose **Options...**

3 Select the **Sending** tab

• If the **Save copies of messages in Sent Items folder** checkbox is selected, a copy of everything you send will be saved automatically in the *Sent Items* folder when you click the **Send** tool. The *Sent Items* folder is displayed in the *Mail* category on the **Outlook Bar**.

4 Select or de-select this option as required

If you are not familiar with Outlook, explore it using the on-line Help, the menus and dialog boxes. You'll find lots of useful features that will try to make you more efficient!

Provided you have a document open in Word, you can e-mail that document directly from Word. The document you have open in Word will become an 'attachment' to your mail message.

To e-mail a document from within Word:

1 Open the document you want to e-mail

2 Choose **Send To** from the **File** menu

3 Select **Mail Recipient...**

• If Outlook is not running, the **Choose Profile** dialog box will appear as the application opens. Select your profile name from the dialog box and click **OK**.

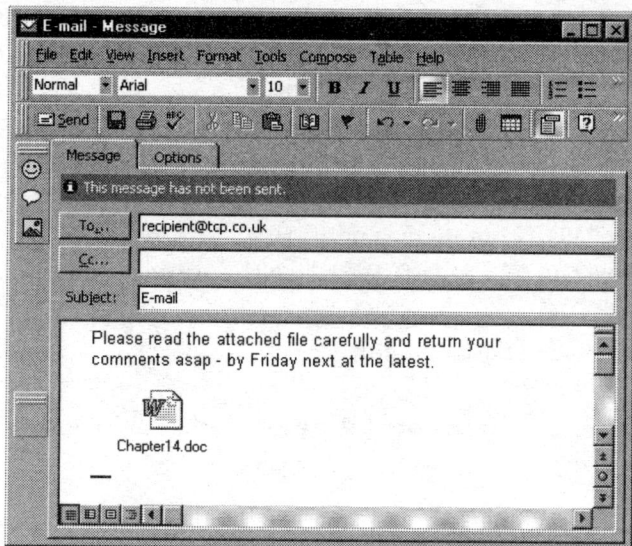

4 Enter the e-mail address you want to send the message to (or click the **To...** button and select the address from the list)

5 Enter or edit the **Subject** as necessary

6 Type in your message

• The current document is an attachment to your mail message

7 Click **Send**

8 Close your message

A record of the items you send is kept in the Sent Items folder in Outlook.

To attach a document from within Outlook:

1 Click the **New Mail Message** tool on the Outlook toolbar

2 Enter the address in the **To** field and **Cc** field if necessary

3 Type in your **Subject**

4 Key in your message

5 Click the **Insert File** tool [icon]

6 Select the file you want to attach

7 Click **OK**

8 Repeat 5 – 7 as required if you want more than one file attached

9 Send your message

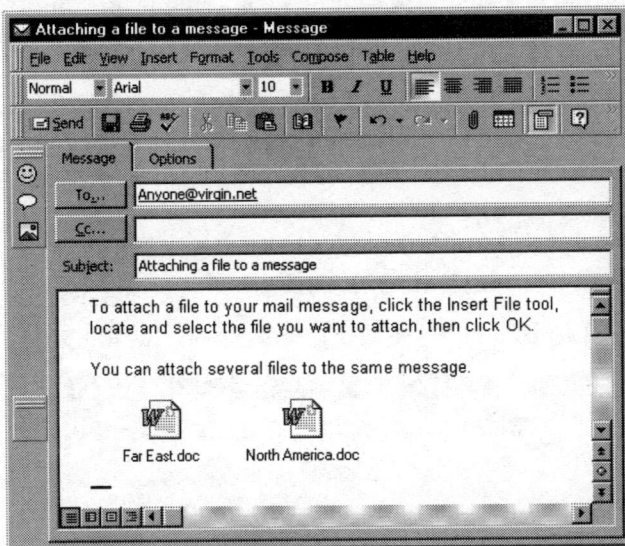

If you send e-mails, you will obviously expect to receive some in return. E-mails that are sent to you appear in your In-Box.

To read an e-mail you receive:

1 Click **Inbox** in the Outlook toolbar

2 Double click on the message you want to read

3 If the message has files attached to it, double click the attachment icon to read the file

You can use the tools on the Outlook toolbar to reply, reply to all, forward, print and delete your e-mail messages.

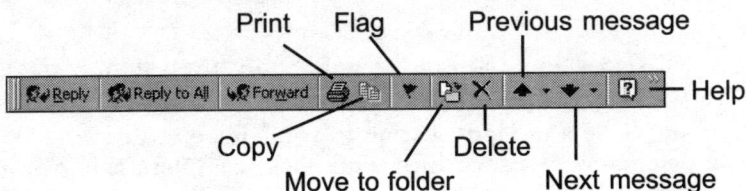

15.3 Hyperlinks

A hyperlink is a 'hot spot' that lets you jump from your document to another location – on your own computer, on your company network or anywhere in world via the Internet.

*   The Internet is a collection of thousands of computer networks that are scattered throughout the world. You can access the data on these computers if you are connected to the Internet.

You can insert a hyperlink anywhere in your document. When you click one, the file that it points to is displayed on your screen.

To insert a hyperlink to a file:

1   Click the **Insert Hyperlink** tool 🖳 on the Standard toolbar

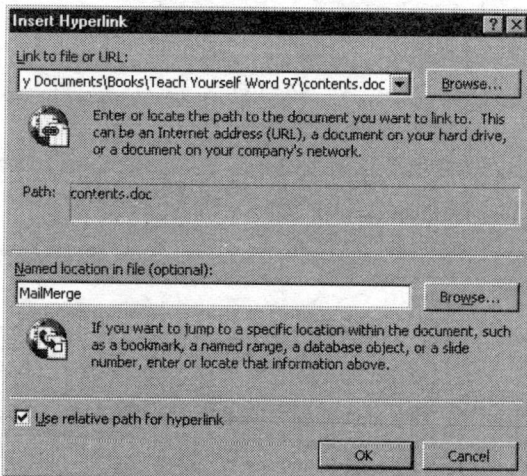

2   Type in the path and name of the file you want to jump to
or

Click **Browse...** and locate the file on your system using the **Link to File** dialog box

3   If you have a named location in your file, e.g. a bookmark in a document or range in a workbook, complete the **Named location in file** field if you want to jump to that point

4 Click **OK**

The hyperlink will be inserted into your document. The text usually appears blue, with a blue underline. The example hyperlink, *contents.doc-MailMerge* jumps to a bookmark called *MailMerge* in a Word document called *contents.doc*.

To insert a hyperlink to an URL on the Web:

1 Click the Insert Hyperlink tool on the Standard toolbar

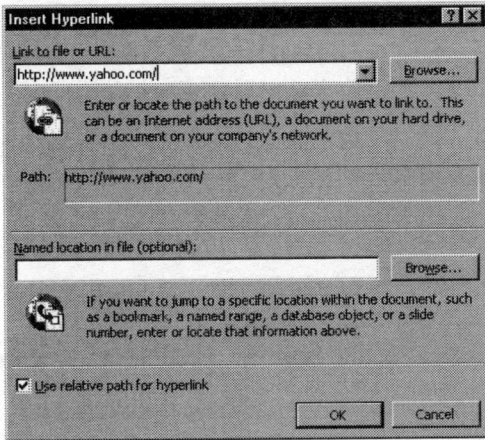

2 Type in the URL (Universal Resource Locator – the address of a Web page or file on the Internet) of the page you want to jump to

or

Click **Browse...** so that you can search the Web

· If you opt to Browse, click the **Search the Web** tool in the **Link to File** dialog box.

3 Locate the page you want to link to

4 Return to Word – click **Microsoft Word** on the Task Bar

5 Click **OK** at the Insert Hyperlink dialog box – your hyperlink field will be inserted, e.g. *http://www.yahoo.com/*

Let's get user-friendly!

In the examples above, the path or URL of the file or page the hyperlink points to is displayed in your document. You may prefer to display a more user-friendly prompt in place of the path or address.

1 Type in the text you want to appear as your hyperlink prompt, e.g. *Go To Yahoo!*
2 Select the text
3 Click the **Insert Hyperlink** tool 🖧 on the Standard toolbar
4 Enter the path or URL (or Browse to locate what you want)
5 Click **OK** at the **Insert Hyperlink** dialog box

The hyperlink has been inserted into your document, with the prompt – Go To Yahoo! – rather than the path or address that it actually points to.

To jump to a hyperlink location:
1 Click on the hyperlink

When you jump to a linked location, the Web toolbar is displayed.

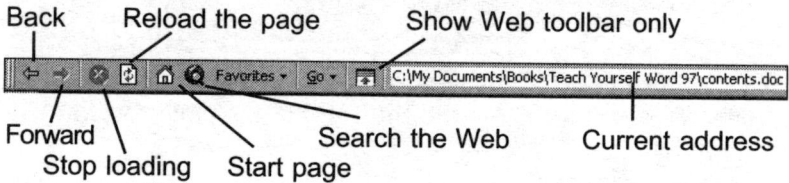

Back   Reload the page   Show Web toolbar only

| ⇦ ⇨ ⊗ 🔄 🏠 🔍 Favorites ▾ Go ▾ 🔲 C:\My Documents\Books\Teach Yourself Word 97\contents.doc |

Forward \   \   Search the Web   Current address
     Stop loading   Start page

If the toolbar doesn't appear, click the **Web toolbar** tool 🌐 on the Standard toolbar. This tool toggles the display of the toolbar.

To return to the document you jumped from, click the **Back** tool.

Once you've jumped to a hyperlink, then returned to your document, the hyperlink field changes colour – usually to violet. This will remind you that you've already used that hyperlink.

To remove a hyperlink:
1 Select the hyperlink in your document
2 Press **[Delete]**

─────15.4 Preparing a Web page─────

The pages you access through the Internet are part of the World Wide Web (affectionately called the Web). You can create your own pages and publish them on the Web if you wish. The easiest way to prepare a page for publication to the Web is using one of the Web Page Wizards. There are several layouts to choose from. Once you've selected a layout, it's simply a case of customising the page with your own details.

To create a page:

1 Open the **File** menu and choose **New**
2 Select the **Web Pages Tab**
3 Choose **Web Page Wizard**
4 Click **OK**
· If the **Connect to the Internet** dialog box appears, click *Yes* or *No*, depending on whether or not you wish to check for a new version of the *Web page authoring tools*. Select the **Don't ask me again** checkbox if you don't want this prompt appearing each time you go to create a Web page.

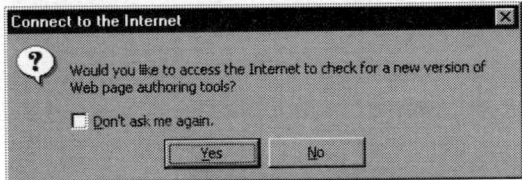

> **Connect to the Internet**
>
> (?) Would you like to access the Internet to check for a new version of Web page authoring tools?
>
> ☐ Don't ask me again.
>
> [Yes]   [No]

5 Select the type of Web page you want to create and click **Next**

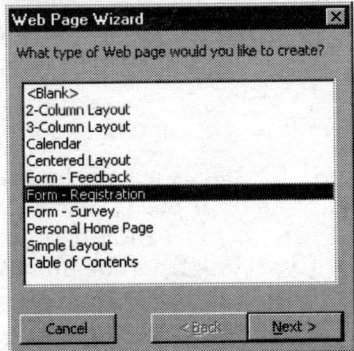

> **Web Page Wizard**
>
> What type of Web page would you like to create?
>
> <Blank>
> 2-Column Layout
> 3-Column Layout
> Calendar
> Centered Layout
> Form - Feedback
> Form - Registration
> Form - Survey
> Personal Home Page
> Simple Layout
> Table of Contents
>
> [Cancel]   [< Back]   [Next >]

6 Choose a **visual style** and
  click **Finish**

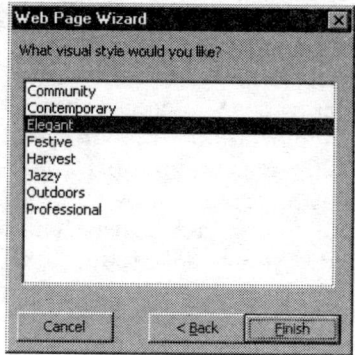

Work through the form that the
wizard creates, replacing and
editing the text as required.

To replace existing text with your own:

1 Select the text you don't want

2 Type in your own

To edit the contents of a Drop-down list:

1 Go into Design Mode – click the **Form Design Mode** tool
  on the Standard toolbar

• The Control toolbox will appear.

2 Select the Drop-down list field on the Web page

3 Click the **Properties** tool on the Control
  toolbox

4 Edit the **DisplayValues** row to display the
  options you want to use (make sure you
  leave a ; between options)

5 Close the **Properties** dialog box

6 Exit Design Mode when you've finished –
  click the **Exit Design Mode** tool on the
  Control toolbox

7 Close the Control toolbox if necessary

• Some pages set up by the wizards have Hyperlink prompts
  already in place. Select the text in these and replace it with
  your own. You can then select each prompt and insert a
  Hyperlink from the prompt to other documents or Web pages.

• Save your Web page – it will be saved as in HTML (HyperText
  Markup Language) format, ready to publish on the Web

Hyperlinks

Drop-down list

WEB PAGE AUTHORING TOOLS

If you have no Web Pages tab in your New dialog box, you may need to run Office Setup again and install the Web page authoring tools – select Web Page Authoring (HTML) in Setup.

To Install Web Page Authoring (HTML):

1 Close any applications that are running – including Word
2 Click **Start** on the Taskbar
3 Select **Settings...**, then **Control Panel**
4 Double click on **Add/Remove Programs**
5 Choose *Microsoft Office 97* or *Microsoft Office 97, Professional Edition* from the list of applications
6 Click **Add/Remove...**
7 Insert the Microsoft Office CD at the prompt and click **OK**
8 Click **Add/Remove...**
9 Select *Web Page Authoring (HTML)*
10 Click **Continue** and follow the prompts on the screen

—15.5 Word documents to Web pages—

If you already have documents saved in Word that you want to publish to the Web, you can easily create an HTML file from your document.

1 Open the document you want to prepare for publication
2 Choose **Save As HTML...** from the **File** menu
3 Complete the **Save As HTML** dialog box – it is virtually the same as the normal **Save As** dialog box.
4 Click **Save**

—— 15.6 Previewing your Web page ——

Once you've created your page, you should preview it before you publish.

To preview your Web page:

1 Click the **Web Page Preview** tool on the Standard toolbar
• Your page will be displayed as it will appear when you publish it on the Web.
2 Check it carefully for spelling and sense – a lot of people may read it
3 Complete the fields with some typical data
4 Test any hyperlinks
5 Close the preview when you've finished – click the **Close** button on the Title Bar
6 Edit your page if necessary, save it and preview again

When you've got the layout correct, save and close your file. You're now ready to publish!

15.7 Publishing to the Web

To publish your HTML file to the Web you must transfer your file from your own computer to a server that is provided by your service provider (unless you want your own computer to become a server on the Web). The server that your service provider has will be switched on 24 hours a day so anyone who knows the URL of your Web page will be able to access it at any time.

Most service providers will allocate some free space to you for your own Web pages – 10 Mb (about 7 diskettes worth) is fairly typical.

There are a number of ways to 'upload' files to a service providers' server – contact your service provider to find out how to upload your files to their server.

If you have created hyperlinks in your Web page that jump to other files on your computer, remember to upload all the files, not just the main page.

15.8 Summary

This final chapter has discussed ways in which you can interact with the wider world from Word. We have discussed how you can:

- Send and receive e-mail messages.
- Create hyperlinks to other files.
- Create hyperlinks to Web pages.
- Display a 'user-friendly' prompt for hyperlinks.
- Create pages for publication to the Web.
- Find out how to publish your Web pages.

——— 15.7 Publishing to the Web ———

To publish your HTML file to the Web you must transfer your file from your own computer to a server that is provided by your service provider (unless you want your own computer to become a server on the Web). The server that your service provider has will be switched on 24 hours a day so anyone who knows the URL of your Web page will be able to access it at any time.

Most service providers will allocate some free space to you for your own Web pages – 10 Mb (about 7 diskettes worth) is fairly typical.

There are a number of ways to 'upload' files to a service providers' server – contact your service provider to find out how to upload your files to their server.

If you have created hyperlinks in your Web page that jump to other files on your computer, remember to upload all the files, not just the main page.

——————— 15.8 Summary ———————

This final chapter has discussed ways in which you can interact with the wider world from Word. We have discussed how you can:

- Send and receive e-mail messages.
- Create hyperlinks to other files.
- Create hyperlinks to Web pages.
- Display a 'user-friendly' prompt for hyperlinks.
- Create pages for publication to the Web.
- Find out how to publish your Web pages.

INDEX